redefining
life: MYRELATIONSHIPS

redefining
life: MYRELATIONSHIPS

A NAVSTUDY FEATURING THE**MESSAGE**®//REMIX™

Written and compiled by Margaret Feinberg

THINK
P.O. Box 35001
Colorado Springs, Colorado 80935

ISBN 1-57683-888-9

Cover design by Kirk DouPonce, DogEaredDesign.com
Cover photo by Matthew Antrobus, Getty
Creative Team: Nicci Jordan, Steve Parolini, Arvid Wallen, Kathy Mosier, Glynese Northam

Written and compiled by Margaret Feinberg

Printed in the United States of America

1 2 3 4 5 6 7 8 9 10 / 09 08 07 06 05

contents

about the redefininglife series

It's in Christ that we find out who we are and
what we are living for.

Ephesians 1:11

For most of your life, you've been a student. And yet in a moment—probably marked by a ceremony—the title you carried for more than a dozen years was stripped away. So now how will you describe yourself when people ask? Are you a professional? An adult? A temporarily unemployed graduate? What seems to fit? Or do any of these fit at all?

Expectations are probably pretty high. But only a few of your graduating class fall into the life you wish you could have—the great job, the wonderful lifelong relationship, the incredible devotion to God. For the rest of you, it's back to square one in many ways. What has been defined for you in the past is suddenly up for negotiation.

The discussion guides in the REDEFINING LIFE series give you a forum to help with that negotiation process. They can help you figure out who you are, *who you really are,* whether you're still taking classes, employed full-time, or somewhere in between. They can help you find out what's really important in life, how to thrive in your work, and how to grow lifelong, meaningful relationships.

REDEFINING LIFE is a place to ask the hard questions of yourself and others. We're talking about a "marrow deep" kind of honesty. At the very least, these discussion guides will show you that you're not alone in the process of self-definition. And hopefully, they will also give you a glimpse—or maybe more—of God's role in the defining of you.

introduction

GOD said, "It's not good for the Man to be alone;
I'll make him a helper, a companion." So GOD formed
from the dirt of the ground all the animals of the
field and all the birds of the air. He brought
them to the Man to see what he would name them.
Whatever the Man called each living creature, that
was its name. The Man named the cattle, named the
birds of the air, named the wild animals; but he
didn't find a suitable companion.

Genesis 2:18-20

Throughout the story of Creation, God looked at His work and saw that it was good. But when God noticed that man was alone, He said, "It's not good." And He made woman. By doing so, He not only instituted the first marriage, but He also created the first family. Friendships were formed, and the bonds among humans began to take all kinds of different forms from roommates to BFF (best friends forever) to romantic relationships.

There's no question that God designed humans for relationship—not only with Himself but also with each other. Unfortunately, relationships are not always easy to navigate. They're rife with pain and uncertainty and miscommunication and all kinds of difficult things. But they're also filled with joy and peace and love and transcendent wonder. They're worth the effort.

In this discussion guide, you are going to be challenged to look closely at your relationships—to examine what's going right and what's not going right and to evaluate how well you're doing in relationships with friends, family, and even that potential (or current) "significant other." This is a place to put pretense aside and be honest about what's going on in your relational life.

Relationships take work. Thankfully, lots of people have been there already and have some good ideas on how to weave through the challenges with some success. Scripture is your best source for relational help, and we've included plenty here for you to wrestle with. You'll also find help from the other readings in this discussion guide.

This study, of course, is best done in a small group. You were *designed* for relationship.

how to
use this
discussion guide

REDEFINING LIFE isn't like any other study. We're not kidding. REDEFINING LIFE isn't designed with easy, obvious-to-answer questions and nice fill-in-the-blanks. It's got more of a wide-open-spaces feel to it.

The process is simple, really. Complete a lesson *on your own* (see details below). Then get with your small group and go through it again *together*. Got it?

Okay, want a little more direction than that? Here you go. And if you want even more help, check out the Discussion Group Study Tips (page 161) and the Frequently Asked Questions (page 163) sections in the back of the book.

1. Read, read, read. Each lesson contains five sections, but don't think of them as homework. This isn't an assignment to be graded. And at the end of the week, you don't have to turn it in to a teacher, professor, or boss. So don't read this as a "have to" but as a "get to." Think about how you read when you're on vacation. Set a leisurely pace. Try to enjoy what you read. Then read it again. Allow the words and meaning to soak in. Use the First Thoughts box to

first thoughts
like:
dislike:
agree:
disagree:
don't get it:

record your initial reactions to the text. (That's a sample on the previous page.) Then use the space provided in and around the reading to make notes. What bugs you? What inspires you? What doesn't make sense? What's confusing? Be honest. Be real. Be yourself. Don't shy away from phrases or sentences you don't understand or don't like. Circle them. Cross them out. Add exclamation marks or smiley faces.

2. Think about what you read. Think about what you wrote. Always ask:

- What does this mean?
- Why does this matter?
- How does this relate to my life right now?
- What does Scripture have to say about this?

Then respond to the questions provided. If you have a knack for asking questions, don't be shy about writing some of your own. You may have a lot to say on one topic, little on another. That's okay. When you come back to the passages in your small group, listen. Allow the experience of others to broaden your understanding and wisdom. You'll be stretched here—called on to evaluate what you've discovered and asked to make practical sense of it. In community, that stretching can often be painful and sometimes even embarrassing. But your willingness to be transparent—your openness to the possibility of personal growth—will reap great rewards. Vulnerability spurs growth in yourself and others.

3. Pray as you go through the entire session—before you begin reading, as you're thinking about a passage and its questions, and especially before you get together in a small group. Pause 'n' pray whenever you need to ask God for help along the way. Prayer takes many forms. You can speak your prayers. Be silent. Write them in the space at the bottom of each page. You can pray a Scripture or a spiritual song. Just don't forget that one of the most important parts of prayer is taking time to listen for God's response.

4. Live. What good are study, reflection, and prayer if they don't lead to action? When reflecting on the week's worth of lessons, think about what impacted you and how you can turn that lesson into action. After studying the issue of forgiveness, you may realize you need to write a letter or email to someone. After studying God's generosity, you may feel compelled to give a gift to a particular outreach. Figure out what God is calling you to do to live out your faith. Sometimes you'll finish a week's worth of lessons and each group member will decide to commit to the same goal. Other times you'll each walk away with a different conviction or goal. Record your goals in the book.

5. Follow up. What good are information and conversation if they don't lead to transformation? Your goal in doing any good study is to ultimately become more like Christ, and this is no exception. Prepare yourself to take your faith and make it active and alive. Be willing to set goals and hold others (as well as be held) accountable in your group. Part of being in a community of Jesus-followers means asking, "Hey, did you do what you said you were going to do?" It will help you put your faith into action as part of a community.

6. Repeat as necessary.

Aug 27
2:19 pm

finding God
on your own

The person who lives in right relationship with God does it by embracing what God arranges for him. Doing things for God is the opposite of entering into what God does for you. Habakkuk had it right: "The person who believes God, is set right by God—and that's the real life."

Galatians 3:11

the defining line

We start every lesson by asking you to do a sometimes-difficult thing: define the core truths about the study topic as it relates to you right now. Use this "beginning place" to set the foundation for the lesson. You can then build, change, adjust, and otherwise redefine your life from here.

Your relationship with God is constantly changing. Some days you feel closer to Him than others. Some days you are more aware of His presence. And some days you clearly see His activity in your life. Though your awareness and perceptions of God may change, He remains the same. How would you describe your relationship with God right now?

I have felt very distant from God in the past
few months. I just spent a long time praying +
talking to God today. I feel so much better. It
is going to have to be a daily (even hourly) thing
that I have to work on.

In the space below, draw a picture that illustrates how close or far away you feel from Him right now.

What is standing in the way of a closer relationship with God? Add that image to the picture you just drew above.

In the space below, draw a picture that illustrates the relationship you *desire* to have with God. Beside that picture, draw an image of the relationship *God* desires to have with you.

Now dig a little deeper. What doubts, fears, or insecurities prevent you from having the kind of relationship with God that your heart desires? What beliefs about God do you know on a mental level but struggle to realize on a heart level?

Doubts

My future
love

Fears

Life

Love

dissapointing people

Insecurities

my image
who I am

Now dig even deeper. What motivates you to grow in your life and in your faith? What compels you to go to work or class every day? What gets you out of bed? Use the space below to describe what really drives you to move forward.

Motivations

To Grow in life * I guess I just have to
To Grow in faith * To know God & feel God
To go to class * To achieve something
To get out of bed * To go to school so
I can finish & not dissapoint myself
or anyone else

Consider sharing your responses with your group when you meet.

read Knowing God

From *The Pursuit of God* by A. W. Tozer[1]

Canon Holmes, of India, more than twenty-five years ago called attention to the inferential character of the average man's faith in God. To most people God is an inference, not a reality. He is a deduction from evidence which they consider adequate, but He remains personally unknown to the individual. "He must be," they say, "therefore we believe He is." Others do not go even so far as this; they know of Him only by hearsay. They have never bothered to think the matter out for themselves, but have heard about Him from others, and have put belief in Him into the back of their minds along with various odds and ends that make up their total creed. To many others, God is but an ideal, another name for goodness or beauty or truth; or He is law or life or the creative impulse back of the phenomena of existence.

These notions about God are many and varied, but they who hold them have one thing in common: They do not know God in personal experience. The possibility of intimate acquaintance with Him has not entered their minds. While admitting His existence they do not think of Him as being knowable in the sense that we know things or people.

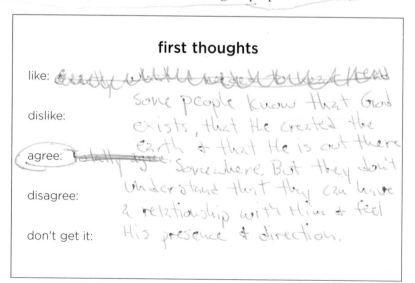

first thoughts

like: *Exactly what I've been thinking*

dislike:

agree: *totally agree* — *Some people know that God exists, that He created the earth & that He is out there somewhere. But they don't understand that they can have a relationship with Him & feel His presence & direction.*

disagree:

don't get it:

think

- The Bible talks about loving God with your whole heart, mind, soul, and strength. With which of these is it easiest for you to love God? With which is it hardest? Why?
- In what ways is God more of an inference than a reality in your life? In what ways do you struggle to know Him personally?
- What makes it so difficult to get to know God? How can you know God through personal experience?
- How have you "bothered to think the matter out" for yourself? What did that process look like?

- Easiest - strength because I am weak. Hardest - Mind because it is everywhere + I try to control it myself.
- I sometimes take advantage of the fact that I know He is a reality. I know He's real + He's there, so I sometimes don't even bother to pay attention to Him or even let myself have the chance to. I struggle to know Him more because I put off praying + talking to Him because I tell myself I have other things to do, and then I get further away from Him.
- I try to control my life myself. There's things that I try not to give over to God, things I want to hold on to. But God doesn't just want pieces of me, He wants all of me. I can know God better if I give Him all of me + pray/talk to Him not just daily, but hourly, even minutely.
- I try to control everything. I think I can do it myself + I can't. The process is always a mess

pray

read Fresh Start

Psalm 32

Count yourself lucky, how happy you must be—
    you get a fresh start,
    your slate's wiped clean.

Count yourself lucky—
    GOD holds nothing against you
    and you're holding nothing back from him.

When I kept it all inside,
    my bones turned to powder,
    my words became daylong groans.

The pressure never let up;
    all the juices of my life dried up.

Then I let it all out;
    I said, "I'll make a clean breast of my failures to GOD."

Suddenly the pressure was gone—
    my guilt dissolved,
    my sin disappeared.

These things add up. Every one of us needs to pray;
    when all hell breaks loose and the dam bursts
    we'll be on high ground, untouched.

GOD's my island hideaway,
    keeps danger far from the shore,
    throws garlands of hosannas around my neck.

Let me give you some good advice;
    I'm looking you in the eye
    and giving it to you straight:

"Don't be ornery like a horse or mule
    that needs bit and bridle
    to stay on track."

God-defiers are always in trouble;
    GOD-affirmers find themselves loved
    every time they turn around.

Celebrate GOD.
    Sing together—everyone!
    All you honest hearts, raise the roof!

---

first thoughts

like: *It's Amazing how God tells you exactly what you need to hear. Even if it's not with His voice, it's with*

dislike: *His Words.*

agree: *HE IS AMAZING*

disagree:

don't get it:

---

think

- In what ways do you struggle to be honest — *really* honest — with God?
- What does it feel like when you get real with God? What is the hardest part? What is the most rewarding part?
- Is there anything you're holding back from God right now? Is there anything you're angry or upset with God about? What is preventing you from being honest with Him?

- About my insecurities. I Guess because I want to hold on to them for myself + not give them fully over to Him.

- I feel a little ashamed but I know it's good to talk to Him about it. Hardest - I feel sometimes like I don't trust Him fully with it. Rewarding - I always feel alot better after I bring it to Him.

- Something I've been holding back for a while but I've just recently started bringing it to Him. I don't think I'm angry or upset with God, but with myself, yes. I want to hold on to certain things + control certain things myself. I'm working on that though.

pray

read Overwhelming Complacency

From "Tips on Surviving Complacency University" by Kate Zorichak[2]

After spending a few semesters abroad, I came back to the main campus of my Christian college for a visit. To my disappointment, friends who were entering their junior year were in the exact same spiritual state they were the first week of freshman orientation. The same shallow questions were being asked of each other, and other than mandatory chapels, my friends had no desire to dive deeper into a personal growth.

I am just as guilty. At one time I sported the complacency U hoodie. My first year at school I slowly sank into a comfortable state of dragging myself to chapel Tuesdays and Thursdays and doing the quick pre-exam prayer: "Lord, please help me do well on this test." When my friends and I really wanted to be spiritual, we would go around asking people, "How can I pray for you?" With little or no desire to actually pray for them, it was almost a way to justify gossiping. "Hey, make sure you pray for Amber . . . she's having problems with alcohol again."

Why are there so many unmotivated and passionless Christians in college? Why have we turned our colleges across the country into "Complacency University?" I strongly believe that it doesn't come down on the college itself, but more on the individuals who attend. Since we assume we are a "Christian," we naturally assume that our environment would reflect our faith. However, we fall into the lie that we've got everything together and that everybody else is on the same page we are. Several people at my school like

first thoughts

like:

dislike:

agree: *I think we use laziness & business as an excuse to put God on the back burner*

disagree:

don't get it:

to call that concept the "bubble." During the school year, we tend to lose all concept of reality and what is going on in the real world.

I am about to graduate in May, and I can't help but think about the time I wasted being lazy with my relationship with Christ and other people.

think

- In what ways do your experiences parallel those described in this article? In what ways are your experiences different?
- How has your relationship with God changed since you've become an adult? In what ways has your faith become your own?
- How have you been tempted to be lazy in your relationships with others? With God? What do you need to do to deepen those relationships?

- Since I started cosmetology school, I've put God on the backburner. Busyness is no excuse. Different - I've never been to college or a christian college, but I know beauty school is alot different than a christian school & christianity isn't really accepted. So that's even more of struggle to pray daily for me.

- I think I've matured alot in my relationship with God. Even though I'm not where I want to be, I've matured enough to realize it & do something to change it.

- I tend to blow people off, not return phone calls, not attempt to relate to others, only because ... well I'm not sure why. I think I need to be comfortable with myself so I can be comfortable around others.

pray

read Honestly God

Matthew 6:5-8

"And when you come before God, don't turn that into a theatrical production either. All these people making a regular show out of their prayers, hoping for stardom! Do you think God sits in a box seat?

"Here's what I want you to do: Find a quiet, secluded place so you won't be tempted to role-play before God. Just be there as simply and honestly as you can manage. The focus will shift from you to God, and you will begin to sense his grace.

"The world is full of so-called prayer warriors who are prayer-ignorant. They're full of formulas and programs and advice, peddling techniques for getting what you want from God. Don't fall for that nonsense. This is your Father you are dealing with, and he knows better than you what you need."

---

first thoughts

like:

dislike:

agree: *Sometimes at church it seems like some of the people who pray are doing it as a show, using big words (of which I don't understand) and using*

disagree: *God @ times + everything. I know there's no wrong way to pray but sometimes it seems like they've rehearsed it.*

don't get it:

---

think

- In what ways do you see others making their relationships with God a "theatrical production"? In what ways are you tempted to do this in your relationship with God?
- In what types of settings do you connect with God best? What prevents you from going to those settings more often?
- Make a list of at least three prayers you've seen God answer in the last year.
- How do you see God working in your life right now?

- The only thing I can think of is sometimes at church when certain people pray. I Guess I sometimes "talk the talk" to others & don't really walk the walk. I Give "spiritual" advice but don't even follow my own advice.

- When I'm alone. Usually when I'm driving, running in the shower, or just alone in my room. I use business (or my anxiety, rather) as an excuse sometimes. I'm working on it.

- My sister to get on the right track with God. Me to have Christian friends at school. Ryan to find a good job & get up on his fe

- He is showing me that I have to trust Him completely with everything & that I need to be comforted by His presence wheth I'm alone or not alone. I am never alone with God on my side.

pray

read Stuck with God

From "The Glory of Being Stuck" by Mike Yaconelli[3]

If I were to diagram my spiritual life, it would look something like this:

A continual series of ups and downs, through all of my life, moving in a slow upward direction, although some of the lows would seem lower than before and some of the highs would seem higher than before.

Me

When I picture this graph, it is not encouraging at first, because the longer I live, the further away the end of the graph appears. It is very much like the elusive end of the rainbow—the closer I get, the further away it seems. And yet . . . yet there is something you cannot see on a one-dimensional diagram, something you cannot express with lines and words. There is a hidden excitement that begins to surface, a tingling of the soul that quickens my consciousness as I gaze at this trail of God in my life. I suddenly realize a great truth—the up-and-down syndrome of my life is the fingerprint of God on my soul! It is the remains of my struggle of faith, the ups and downs of my ongoing dialogue with the Father. It is the way growth looks.

I am beginning to realize that the spiritual life is not so much progress as it is *process*. It is not a continuous climb *upward* as much as it is a continuous *climb*. It is not the victories that matter so much as the *going on after the defeats*. The longer the erratic dance of faith goes on, the less you care about what God is doing, and the more you want to know about God. Spirituality is, after all, about intimacy with God.

Look at the graph for a minute. Notice the low spots—flat, long at times, surrounded by highs. Whatever the low spots are, they appear to be negative. If the high spots represent the "good" or "positive" in my spiritual life and the low spots represent the "bad" or "negative" in my relationship with God, then obviously the high spots are to be sought after and the lows are to be avoided.

But what if we do something radical? What if we remove those kind of value judgments from this graph? What if, in place of concepts like good and bad, positive and negative, high and low, we replace our value judgments with words like "stalled" and "moving," or "listening" and "acting," or "stopping" and "starting," or "waiting" and "not waiting"? What does that do to our understanding of the spiritual life? Maybe waiting is "good" and not waiting is "bad." Maybe stopping is better than starting, listening better than acting, and stalling better than moving. Maybe one cannot happen without the other. Maybe stopping is necessary to starting, maybe acting cannot happen without listening first.

Of course, I do not believe there is any "maybe" about it. I believe that our understanding of spirituality has been distorted and ruined by our artificial judgments and our one-dimensional understanding of our relationship with God.

Let me point out a couple of interesting characteristics of this graph. Every high is followed by a low and every high is preceded by a low. Maybe what the graph means is that you cannot achieve a high without first achieving a low. Maybe lows are not low at all, but just part of the highs. I would like to abandon the high/low model and rename these parts as "stuck" and "unstuck." Maybe, getting stuck is necessary before we can get unstuck . . . which means that getting stuck is actually a wonderful place to be.

When you look at it like this, then getting stuck is not only a necessary part of spirituality, it is a prerequisite to spiritual growth.

Most of the Church considers being stuck a negative, a sin of failure or burn-out, an indication that a person isn't working hard enough on their spiritual life. It's a report card on personal Bible reading and prayer, and the grade is F. If you feel stuck in your spiritual life, then you aren't doing something right *because no one should be stuck with God.*

Nothing could be more untrue. The truth is that *everyone should be stuck with God many times because it is the prerequisite to being unstuck.*

Being stuck is a great moment. It may be characterized by frustration, loneliness, or detachment, but those things are only the vocabulary of our souls telling us we are in danger. It is the cry of our souls craving for more. It is our longings and yearnings trying to get our attention. It is a summons, a call from within. It is the glorious music of disaffection and dissatisfaction with where we are now. It is the anguish of our interior life pleading with us—not to give up, but to give *in*. It is the Holy Spirit stopping us dead in our tracks so we can read the words that God has written on our hearts—surrender.

Surrender.

Put your arms around your soul, embrace your anguish, respond to your summons from God. Get ready for the adventure of growing on to the next part of your life. Getting stuck is worth whatever anguish you must go through just so you can hear God say to you, "Hang on, you are about to get unstuck."

---

first thoughts

like: *"Hang on, you are about to get unstuck".*

dislike:

agree: *The first thing I've heard in a long time that's actually made sence to me.*

disagree:

don't get it:

---

think

- Respond to this statement: "Being stuck is a great moment."
- Draw a diagram of your relationship with God over the past year. At what points did you lean into God for His protection and provision? At what points did you lean away from Him?
- Describe a moment when you were stuck in your relationship with God. What events preceded it? What events followed it? How did you feel about God during that time? How did you feel about yourself?
- Why do you think God allows so many "high" and "low" moments in our relationships with Him?

- In order to be unstuck you must first be stuck, resulting in spiritual growth.

Jan Feb March Apr May June July Aug
(started school, moved
out, lived with a crazy
girl)
10.
9.
8.   Leaned on Him
7.   (moved back
6.   home, became
5.   downfall   bitter) (Now)
4.   i'm on my way up!
3.
2.
1.

- When I moved out of my appartment I was bitter & angry & confused. I stopped praying & started to not trust myself or God as much. I trusted alot & prayed alot before I started school & moved out. I felt out of control of my life so I needed His guidence. I felt good about my decisions for moving in with Rebecca & going to school. Then everything started to crumble & I doubted everything.

pray
- Maybe so that we grow closer to Him through our lows. Maybe knowing what our "highs" feel like bring us out of our lows.

redefininglife

live   The Redefining

Take a few moments to skim through the notes you've made in these readings. What do they tell you about how you view your relationship with God? Based on what you've read and discussed, are there any areas of your relationship with God that you need to be more intentional about?

when things are out of control, I turn to Him. Afterwards I tend to have bitter & angry feelings & kind of ignore God & His word. I need to stop doing that.

Do you have any unhealthy views of God? How are they affecting your relationship with Him? What can you do to replace those views with a healthier perspective of who God really is?

what I wrote above. Also I sometimes feel like if I give Him certain things that He is going to give me what I don't want to make me appreciate Him more. It's a little confusing to explain. Read His word & pray for help to understand it. Just pray in general, talk with God.

What steps do you need to take to cultivate a more intimate relationship with God?

Pray, Pray, Pray. Trust, Trust, Trust. Repent, Repent, Repent.

What, if anything, is holding you back?

For a long time, trust. I've been working on it alot though. I know I've said that alot but I have.

What can you do in the upcoming months to get to know God better?

Keep praying & listening for His guidence. Don't try to run your own show. God is the director.

Talk with a close friend about all of the above. Brainstorm together about what it might take to move toward God in this area of your life. Determine what this looks like in a practical sense and then list any measurable goals you want to shoot for here. Review these goals each week to see how you're doing.

- Pray when you're stuck
- Pray when you're frustrated
- Pray even when you don't want to
- Thank God
- Praise God
- Know He has everything under control.
- Constantly remind yourself He is in control
- Give everything to Him, by the minute.
- Know you are not alone

true
friends

Friends come and friends go,
    but a true friend sticks by you like family.

Proverbs 18:24

a reminder

Before you dive into this study, spend a little time reviewing what you wrote in the previous lesson's Live section. How are you doing? Check with your small-group members and review your progress toward the specified goals. If necessary, adjust your goals and plans and then recommit to them.

the defining line

It's been said that a friend is someone you can think out loud around. Real friends encourage you to be yourself. They accept you for who you are—complete with weaknesses and faults—and love you anyway. Together, your friends provide a network to support you through tough times and celebrate with you during good times. Your friends may be more valuable than you realize. In the space below, make a list of reasons why friendships are so important. Share your list with the discussion group.

They are honest with you when you aren't thinking clearly. They help you to make decisions when your vision is cloudy. You lift each other up. You can't on each other.

redefininglife

What would you say are the three most important characteristics of a good friend? Why are these characteristics so important?

Trust - You need trust for any friendship / relationship
Honesty - If you're not honest, there's no trust
Laughter - Everyone needs to laugh in order to live

Do you tend to seek out friends with the characteristics you listed above, or do you tend toward friends with other characteristics? Why do you think that is true of you?

I have three best friends.
My Sister, Jenna, & Ryan. No specific order.
Just the order in which I meet them.
I trust all three with my life.

In what ways do you reflect the characteristics you listed?

I'm sure I need to work on all the things I listed. I'm not always a reliable friend.

Consider sharing your responses with your group when you meet.

read Superfriends

From "Tribal Culture: Single But Not Alone, These Urbanites Are Redefining the 'Adultescent' Years" by Caroline Hsu[1]

Dawn Trautman was in bad shape. Run ragged by studying for the GREs, holding down a full-time job, and choreographing a high school musical, she had a nasty case of pneumonia that would land her in bed for over a month. But Trautman, 31, who was living alone in a St. Paul, Minn., condo, didn't miss a single meal while she was sick. Although her parents live nearby, it was her friends who kept her nourished, bringing orange juice, making chicken noodle soup, even feeding her in bed when she couldn't get up.

These aren't just friends—they're superfriends. Whether it's a leaky faucet, a broken-down car, a cross-country move, or just lunch, Trautman's group is there, blurring the line between friendship and kinship with gestures large and small. The core group—seven men and women all in their early 30s, including a doctor, a few teachers, and a scientist—volunteer together for political candidates, share gourmet meals, and even vacation as a gang every August. "We've become sort of an urban family," says Trautman.

Groups like Trautman's—less social circles than quasi-familial clans, with their own customs and rituals—are increasingly common, says San Francisco journalist Ethan Watters. They've grown out of well-documented societal change: Where once people got married after high school or college and began building families in their early 20s, men and women today are as likely to stay single for years. According to the 2002 census, the median age at first marriage has risen to 25.3 for women, the highest ever, and 26.9 for men.

In his new book, *Urban Tribes: A Generation Redefines Friendship, Family, and Commitment*, Watters writes that men and women are now structuring the long stretch of single years by gathering in tight-knit clusters—the "urban tribes" of his title. More than casual groups of friends, these are entities that form over time, eventually taking on a life of their own. Often there are rituals, like weekly dinners, yearly group trips, and elaborate theme parties. Many members say there are enough events on the group calendar to fill seven nights a week. "As you get to know people better and get involved in other parts of their lives, you start acting as a group with an inherent organizational structure," says Charles Bradley, 32, who belongs to a 110-member clan in Denver.

---

first thoughts

like:

dislike:

agree:

disagree:

don't get it: I don't get it

---

think

- Have you ever been part of an urban tribe? If so, what was it like? What made your group distinct?
- Why do you think urban tribes are becoming more common in this generation?
- What are some of the qualities or characteristics that make up a healthy urban tribe? What can make a group become unhealthy?

- In what ways do you find your friends "blurring the line between friendship and kinship with gestures large and small"? How does this reflect Christlikeness?

— Sometimes I feel like they don't understand my reasoning for things, and end up guilt trippping me. But I don't blame them. I don't understand my reasons for things sometimes either.

pray

read Embraced by Silence

Job 2:11-13

Three of Job's friends heard of all the trouble that had fallen on him. Each traveled from his own country—Eliphaz from Teman, Bildad from Shuhah, Zophar from Naamath—and went together to Job to keep him company and comfort him. When they first caught sight of him, they couldn't believe what they saw—they hardly recognized him! They cried out in lament, ripped their robes, and dumped dirt on their heads as a sign of their grief. Then they sat with him on the ground. Seven days and nights they sat there without saying a word. They could see how rotten he felt, how deeply he was suffering.

---

first thoughts

like: There's a best friend

dislike:

agree:

disagree:

don't get it:

---

think

- Have you ever had a Job-like experience? If so, describe it.
- Who was there for you through the hardship? Whose actions were the most uplifting during that time?
- Have you found people who will simply sit in silence with you when your world falls apart? Why is silence sometimes more comforting than words?
- In what ways can friendships bring healing in hard times? In what ways can friends actually let you down during hard times?
- Why is it so hard to respond to others appropriately during difficult times?

- Yes, I suppose I have them all the time. When I just need a friend to be there.
  - when my grandma Kathy died.
- My mom and dad. They comforted me.
- Yes, my parents, sister, Ryan, and Jenna. Silence is comforting because sometimes through hard times, there are no words to say to explain the situation. If someone tries, it only makes it worse. There is a comforting feeling of sitting in silence with people you care about, because you are all sharing the same thoughts and emotions, without words to confirm it.
- They can be there for you and let you know they care. Be strong for you when you are weak. They can let you down by not proving to be there when you are hurting.
- Because you want to help them but you don't know what to say or if you're going to say the wrong thing

pray

read The Health Behind Friendships

From "The Dangers of Loneliness" by Hara Estroff Marano[2]

Friendship is a lot like food. We need it to survive. What is more, we seem to have a basic drive for it. Psychologists find that human beings have fundamental need for inclusion in group life and for close relationships. We are truly social animals.

The upshot is, we function best when this social need is met. It is easier to stay motivated, to meet the varied challenges of life.

In fact, evidence has been growing that when our need for social relationships is not met, we fall apart mentally and even physically. There are effects on the brain and on the body. Some effects work subtly, through the exposure of multiple body systems to excess amounts of the hormones of stress. Yet the effects are distinct enough to be measured over time, so that unmet social needs take a serious toll on health, eroding our arteries, creating high blood pressure, and even undermining learning and memory.

A lack of close friends and a dearth of broader social contact generally bring the emotional discomfort or distress known as loneliness. It begins with an awareness of a deficiency of relationships. This cognitive awareness plays through our brain with an emotional soundtrack. It makes us sad. We might feel an emptiness. We may be filled with a longing for contact. We feel isolated, distanced from others, deprived. These feelings tear away at our emotional well-being.

Despite the negative effects of loneliness, it can hardly be considered abnormal. It is a most normal feeling. Everyone feels lonely sometimes—after a break-up with a friend or lover, when we move to a new place, when we are excluded from some social gathering.

Chronic loneliness is something else entirely. It is one of the surest markers in existence for maladjustment.

In adults, loneliness is a major precipitant of depression and alcoholism. And it increasingly appears to be the cause of a range of medical problems, some of which take decades to show up.

Psychologist John Cacioppo of the University of Chicago has been tracking the effects of loneliness. Recently he performed a series of novel studies and reported that loneliness works in some surprising ways to compromise health.

- Perhaps most astonishing, in a survey he conducted, doctors themselves confided that they provide better or more complete medical care to patients who have supportive families and are not socially isolated.

- Living alone increases the risk of suicide for young and old alike.

- Lonely individuals report higher levels of perceived stress even when exposed to the same stressors as nonlonely people, and even when they are relaxing.

- The social interactions lonely people do have are not as positive as those of other people, hence the relationships they have do not buffer them from stress as relationships normally do.

- Loneliness raises levels of circulating stress hormones and levels of blood pressure. It undermines regulation of the circulatory system so that the heart muscle works harder and the blood vessels are subject to damage by blood flow turbulence.

- Loneliness destroys the quality and efficiency of sleep, so that it is less restorative, both physically and psychologically. They wake up more at night and spend less time in bed actually sleeping than do the nonlonely.

Loneliness, Cacioppo concludes, sets in motion a variety of "slowly unfolding pathophysiological processes." The net result is that the lonely experience higher levels of cumulative wear and tear.

In other words, we are built for social contact. There are serious—life-threatening—consequences when we don't get enough. We can't stay on track mentally. And we are compromised physically. Social skills are crucial for your health.

---

first thoughts

like: I want to hang out!

dislike:

agree:

disagree: I'm sure those problems are caused by more than just loneliness.

don't get it:

---

think

- What surprises you most about this study on loneliness?
- How does this passage affect the way you think about your relationships with others? How does it affect the way you reach out and respond to others?
- Have you ever gone through a transitional period when you struggled to make friends? If so, describe it.

- What was the most difficult part of that season?
- Is there anyone you need to reach out to as a friend? What is stopping you?

- Well I definately know + think I need to spend more time with friends. I've been blowing people off because I want to hang out with Ryan. But I know I need to hang out with friends too.

- Not struggled making friends. Just struggled keeping in touch. And still struggling.

- My own issues and wants.

pray

read Broken Friendships

Psalm 41

Dignify those who are down on their luck;
    you'll feel good—*that's* what GOD does.
GOD looks after us all,
    makes us robust with life—
Lucky to be in the land,
    we're free from enemy worries.
Whenever we're sick and in bed,
    GOD becomes our nurse,
    nurses us back to health.

I said, "GOD, be gracious!
    Put me together again—
    my sins have torn me to pieces."
My enemies are wishing the worst for me;
    they make bets on what day I will die.
If someone comes to see me,
    he mouths empty platitudes,
All the while gathering gossip about me
    to entertain the street-corner crowd.
These "friends" who hate me
    whisper slanders all over town.
They form committees
    to plan misery for me.

The rumor goes out, "He's got some dirty,
    deadly disease. The doctors
    have given up on him."

Even my best friend, the one I always told everything
    —he ate meals at my house all the time!—
    has bitten my hand.

GOD, give grace, get me up on my feet.
>   I'll show them a thing or two.

Meanwhile, I'm sure you're on my side—
>   no victory shouts yet from the enemy camp!
You know me inside and out, you hold me together,
>   you never fail to stand me tall in your presence
>   so I can look you in the eye.

Blessed is GOD, Israel's God,
>   always, always, always.
>   Yes. Yes. Yes.

1|21|10

first thoughts

like: God is the best friend anyone cold ever have

dislike:

agree:

disagree:

don't get it:

think

- What does it mean to "dignify those who are down on their luck"? In a practical sense, what does that look like?
- In what ways are friendships, by their very nature, risky?
- When friends fail you, how do you respond? Who do you turn to?
- Describe a moment when someone betrayed you. How did you feel? How did you respond?
- Describe a moment when you betrayed someone else. What prompted the situation? How was it resolved?
- How do you reconcile broken friendships?

- I'm not sure I understand that verse.

- Friendship can be risky 1. by the way you choose your friends. The people you associate with have a big part in the way you view life & your attitude towards everything. 2. We are all human. Friends are going to hurt friends.

- Me personally? Badly. If a friend fails me I am very hurt. I need to turn to God

- I felt betrayed when Jenna lied to me. Or didn't tell the complete truth. I responded with sadness & anger.

- I wasn't there for her when her and my frie broke up.

pray

- Communication.

read The Tests of Friendship

From "I'll Be There" by Ellen J. Langer[3]

When we're down and troubled and we need a helping hand ... we often contemplate the meaning of friendship. The common belief is that when times are tough, true friends are there. But I think those times are the easiest tests of friendship.

In one interesting study on helping, participants were instructed to give a person clues—some easy, others hard—to help that person complete a task. When the task was described as a game, participants gave easier clues to friends than to strangers. However, when the task was presented as serious, participants were more likely to help a stranger than a friend.

Sadly, too often we feel threatened by the successes of our friends, particularly if we are uncomfortable with ourselves. Strangers don't threaten us this way. Moreover, being kind to strangers helps us think well of ourselves and overlook the subtle ways we may have mistreated a friend.

If I am prone to competing with a friend and that friend is in trouble, then, crassly speaking, I am "one up." Anyone who listens to another's woes can feel one up or superior, which is why it is reasonably easy to find a sympathetic ear. This is similar to feeling good when helping someone; the helper is superior to the person in need. My remarks are not meant to belittle the kindnesses we extend to each other in times of need. Instead, they highlight a feature often overlooked when considering a friendship: Can this "friend" be truly happy for us?

It's easy to say, "I'm very happy for you." But how can we tell when the speaker is sincere? We might test this by sharing only good news for a short time. Can this person listen to these details? Is it easy for us to share them? If not, it may be because we are subtly trained to complain. Let me explain by way of example.

I recently went on a wonderful trip that gave me many exciting stories. On the downside, my pocketbook was stolen at the airport on my return home. After my initial negative feelings subsided, I was not as bothered by the theft as one might think, given the way this negative information figured into my stories. I felt some listeners might more easily share my enthusiasm about the trip if they were also given this negative information. But upon reflection, this idea made me sad. I questioned why I exaggerated my bad feelings with some people. It was not premeditated; instead, all of the subtle nonverbal cues I received from them in these few conversations led me in this direction. I did not, however, do this with my closest friends — they were clearly just happy for me.

Reexperiencing our joys in the telling of them should not diminish those joys — it reduces the original experiences. The effect is very subtle: When we complain, the listener seems so comforting that it can be difficult to recognize the negative dynamic that may be operating. The listener, too, may be oblivious given the supportive frame for the consoling interaction. It gives new meaning to the saying, "A friend in need, is a friend indeed." Ironically, the complainer is the friend in deed.

In my view, a real friend can be happy for someone independent of his or her own life experience. We may be able to do this if we don't compete with or envy others. We may also be more likely to put competitiveness and envy aside by recognizing that the relationship is not zero-sum: one winner and one loser. This stance — that the more one has, the less the other has — unwittingly robs both parties. Sharing someone's happiness can be its own positive experience and enable us to enjoy and relive it together. Attention to this mutual, positive need will likely be noticed and, in the long run, better serve the friendship.

Just think about it: Wouldn't it be nice to have a friend, indeed, support this need?

---

first thoughts

like:

dislike:

agree: *There is alot of competitiveness (?) in friendships*

disagree:

don't get it:

think

- Do you think this article has merit? Why or why not? In what ways can you relate to what this article says?
- Has competition—either yours or someone else's—ever undermined one of your friendships? If so, describe the situation.
- What is healthy about competition? What is unhealthy about competition?
- What kinds of people are the hardest to be sincerely happy for?
- What can you do to truly celebrate others' joys?

- I think sometimes we are sidetracked with our jealousness and just need to be happy for our friends. ~~and~~
- Oh yes. It's a daily thing really. Looks, things, relationships, ect.
- I think it's healthy if it's minimal. It makes you strive to be better. It's unhealthy if it is a lot and all your friendship consists of is competing against each other in every situation.
- I guess people who you know don't deserve it. It's not my place to judge, and no one "deserves" anything.

pray

Put aside your jealousy and celebrate with them. Especially if it's a close friend

live   The Redefining

Take a few moments to skim through the notes you've made in these readings. What do they tell you about the importance of friendships in your life? Based on what you've read and discussed, what changes do you need to make to grow or maintain healthy friendships?

Stop competing. Be positive and happy for your friends accomplishments or changes in their life. If they're happy, you're happy

Are there any areas in which you could become a better friend to others? What, if anything, is holding you back?

Just what I said above

Do you have any unhealthy expectations of your friends? Is there anyone you need to forgive or rekindle a friendship with?

I sometimes expect unrealistic things from my friends.

What steps do you need to take to become more Christlike in your friendships?

Make God the center of every relationship and put them in God's hands

What can you do in the upcoming months to be more intentional about deepening your friendships? What can you do to build authentic community among those you know?

Spend more 1 on 1 time with them

Talk with a close friend about all of the above. Brainstorm together about what it might take to move toward God in this area of your life. Determine what this looks like in a practical sense and then list any measurable goals you want to shoot for here. Review these goals each week to see how you're doing.

transitions
with parents

Respect your father and mother—God, your God,
commands it! You'll have a long life; the land
that God is giving you will treat you well.

Deuteronomy 5:16

a reminder

*Before you dive into this study, spend a little time reviewing what
you wrote in the previous lessons' Live sections. How are you doing?
Check with your small-group members and review your progress
toward the specified goals. If necessary, adjust your goals and plans
and then recommit to them.*

the defining line

Mark Twain once wrote, "When I was a boy of 14, my father was so ignorant
I could hardly stand to have the old man around. But when I got to be 21, I
was astonished at how much the old man had learned in seven years."

It's amazing how perceptions of parents change over time. As you've
grown older, there's a good chance that your relationship with your parents
has changed, and it will likely continue to change as you transition from
dependence to independence. Living on your own, being responsible for
your own financial situation, and making decisions completely independent
from your parents can mean major adjustments—for both you and them.
No matter where you are in this transition, it's important to do everything you
can to maintain a healthy relationship with your parents. Sometimes that's

easier said than done. In the space below, describe your current relationship with them. What does it look like?

Over all I think I have a good relationship with my parents. We have our arguments or dissagreements every now and again but it is short lived.

What do you have in common with your parents? What draws you together? What stands in the way of having a closer relationship?

Mom and I have alot in common. Interests, emotions, ways we deal with things, ect. Dad and I have alot of the same interests and we are both organized and opperate very similarly.

In what ways are you becoming independent from your parents?

As I'm getting older I've been making my own decisions and forming my own views and oppinions about things.

Consider sharing your responses with your group when you meet.

read Troublesome Transitions

From the *ABC News* report "Parents Struggle with Letting Go of College Kids: As Teens Leave Home, Baby Boomer Parents Can't Seem to Say Goodbye"[1]

When Katie Ourada headed off to the University of Minnesota this fall, she knew she'd have to juggle classes, homework, friends and new responsibilities. What she didn't expect was how much time she'd have to devote to her parents.

"Most of my communication with my parents, especially my mom, is for her, because I think she's lonely and sad sometimes that I'm not there," said Katie.

According to a recent UCLA survey, 26 percent of college freshman say they speak to their parents every day.

Even with a 10-year-old son still at home, Lisa and Bob Ourada, like many baby boomer parents, have had a very difficult time letting go.

"I sort of prepared myself for this for 18 years—I always dreamed that she would go to college," said Lisa. "And I knew it would be difficult. . . . I guess you can't feel that emptiness until you experience it."

And technology makes it all too easy for them to bridge the 200-mile gap.

The Ouradas call Katie's cell phone at least four times a week, e-mail her two or three times a day and chat via instant messenger for hours on end. Katie sends papers for her mom to proofread and gets care packages from home.

But that's still not enough for mom—who is considering a drastic move.

"I would be willing to move closer to Katie, especially if she would want that also," said Lisa. "I think we're just so connected. More so now than ever."

Marjorie Savage, the parent program director at the University of Minnesota and the author of "You're on Your Own, But I'm Here if You Need Me: A Guide to Parenting College Kids," says there are risks with staying too connected.

"The risk of having a parent be overly involved is that students won't be able to learn how to make decisions, and that really is the biggest thing that students need to be able to do," said Savage.

She said that parents today are having trouble letting go for a number of reasons.

"First of all, parents have been told to be involved since their kids started preschool," she said. "Second, they're investing a lot. College is expensive today. Finally, they're involved because they can be. Communication is instant and constant."

first thoughts

like: I can relate to this

dislike:

agree:

disagree: I don't think it's hard for the parents because they are investing alot. That comes 6 months after they

don't get it: graduate when they realize the extent of the investement

think

- Have you had to draw any boundaries with your parents? If so, describe them.
- In what ways have you been able to maintain a healthy relationship with your parents now that you're on your own? Are there any unhealthy patterns in your relationship? What has stopped you from confronting them?
- What should a healthy relationship between a parent and an adult child look like?
- Do you have any unresolved issues with either of your parents that are affecting your relationship with them today? What is stopping you from resolving those issues?

- I guess so. I've Had to learn how to tell my mom no, or to let her know I'm making my own decisions.

- I'm not really "on my own" yet. I mean I practically am cuz I'm never home, but I'm not quite there yet.

- Be there for each other. Take care of each other. Talk openly and have adult conversations. Talk to your child (adult) like an adult and talk to your parents as an adult.

- There are a few things I'd like to talk with my mom about. My own issues and being cowardly are what is stopping me.

pray

read Honoring Mom and Dad

Ephesians 6:1-4

Children, do what your parents tell you. This is only right. "Honor your father and mother" is the first commandment that has a promise attached to it, namely, "so you will live well and have a long life."

Fathers, don't exasperate your children by coming down hard on them. Take them by the hand and lead them in the way of the Master.

---

first thoughts

like:

dislike:

agree:

disagree:

don't get it:

---

think

- Why do you think God doesn't place a time limit or any exceptions on the command to "honor your father and mother"?
- Why do you think there is a connection between honoring your parents, and living well and having a long life?
- Why is God so concerned with the relationships between parents and their children?
- Do you think the command to honor your parents applies to stepparents? Why or why not?
- Does the way you view or interact with your earthly father affect the way you view your heavenly Father? Explain.

pray

read Boomeranging

From "Hard Times Drive Adult Kids 'Home': Parents Grapple with Rules for 'Boomerangers'" by Linda Greider[2]

In the ad, a slack-jawed 20-something with a three-day growth of beard growls to his parents about the lack of services in their (and his) home, while a cackling grandmother watches from the sidelines. "Whaddaya think this is?" the mother finally asks. "A Holiday Inn?"

While its tone may be exaggerated, the ad does reflect another reality: With the country in tough economic times, more young American adults, over age 18, are returning to the family nest. Some "boomerang" kids may rotate in and out for years, if not decades, changing, for better or worse, the household's dynamics.

And psychologists and other experts say they think terrorist threats may propel more kids toward home.

Many of her young clients, says Mary E. Hotvedt, a Tucson, Ariz., family therapist who is president-elect of the American Association for Marriage and Family Therapy, "have expressed the desire to stay closer to home, closer to family. The reaction is not one necessarily born of fear" but of the need to be with "those emotionally closest to them."

But it's financial pressures that are most likely to send grown children back to the nest. Michael, 28, for example, moved from Michigan to his parents' home north of Phoenix last summer after he lost his job and his marriage failed. He intends to stay just until he can get back on his feet.

Anna, 25, a college student with a part-time job, moved in with her parents in Kensington, Md., last June. "She was having trouble making ends meet," says her mother Patricia. "It's hard to pay for health insurance, student loans and rent on part-time pay."

Historically, the number of boomerang kids rises when the economy turns sour. Under 8 percent of adult children ages 25 to 34 lived with parents in 1970, but the rate began to climb with the lagging economy in the early 1980s, then flattened out in the high-flying dot-com days of the 1990s.

By 2000, when the economy again started to decline, nearly 4 million, or

10.5 percent of the 25 to 34 age group (and 12 percent of those ages 25 to 29) were living in the family home.

"[Today's] students have taken on debt with student loans and credit card bills," says Ken Ramberg, senior vice president of Monstertrak.com, an online consulting and job placement firm. Jobs are hard to get now and harder to keep, he adds, and "young people have seen no loyalty from employers."

Those prospects are driving many students home. A November survey by Monstertrak.com found that 60 percent of current college students plan to move back home after graduation—more than 20 percent plan to stay for at least a year.

Getting married later or working to pay for college can also keep kids at home. So can protective baby boomer parents. They "want to guide their children," says Barbara Coulon of Youth Intelligence, a market research firm. "They want their children to pursue their passion, not simply track down the highest-paying job."

The circumstances under which young people return to the family home range from blissful to desperate. A good outcome for everyone, experts say, depends on a family dynamic that was relatively healthy in the first place, and on clear communication and planning.

Occasionally the dynamic is disastrous, like the Cleveland couple who can't get their grown child to budge now that he's parked in the family home.

"I finally suggested they sell their house and move," says Donald K. Freedheim, a Cleveland clinical psychologist who advised the family. "Of course they couldn't do it."

first thoughts

like:

dislike:

agree:

disagree:

don't get it:

Freedheim has also seen desperate parents threaten to throw their kids' stuff out on the lawn.

Most boomerang families aren't so dysfunctional, and many live in a peaceful, if temporary, state of balance.

think

- Why do you think so many twentysomethings are living with their parents? How is this different from earlier generations?
- Do you think the stigma associated with moving back in with Mom and Dad is increasing or decreasing? Why?
- What should a twentysomething do to make sure the transition to living with his or her parents is as smooth as possible? Make a list of the issues that should be discussed.
- What circumstances have compelled you to either move back in with your parents or avoid it altogether?

pray

read

Enabling Parents

From _Mom, Can I Move Back in with You? A Survival Guide for Parents of Twenty-Somethings_ by Linda Perlman Gordon and Susan Morris Shaffer[3]

Enabling occurs when parents try to protect their children from consequences of their actions, and thereby, fail to hold them accountable for their personal behavior. Enabling parents assume responsibilities that their children should assume for themselves. By engaging in enabling behavior, parents encourage their children to behave less masterly and to be more dependent. Parents shortchange their children when they do things for them that children can do themselves. Inadvertently, they deny their children opportunities to learn a crucial adult skill—to be held accountable for their behavior. Enabling parents give their adult children the unintended message that they don't have faith in their ability to do things themselves.

Enabling parental behavior can be as overt as always bailing a child out of financial difficulties or as subtle as making plane reservations or researching information on the Internet without being asked to do so. Overdoing encourages twentysomethings' irresponsibility, dependency, and lack of self-esteem. In contrast, supportive parenting is a positive form of assistance that encourages children to develop the skills of adulthood.

first thoughts

like:

dislike:

agree:

disagree:

don't get it:

think

- Do any of your friends have enabling parents? Without naming names, how do these parents short-circuit their son's or daughter's personal growth and development?
- In what areas do you feel that your parents enable you? What are some of the unhealthy results?
- How can you break the pattern of being enabled?
- Who do you tend to enable? In what areas do you need to stop enabling someone else?

pray

read Running Home

Luke 15:11-32

Then he said, "There was once a man who had two sons. The younger said to his father, 'Father, I want right now what's coming to me.'

"So the father divided the property between them. It wasn't long before the younger son packed his bags and left for a distant country. There, undisciplined and dissipated, he wasted everything he had. After he had gone through all his money, there was a bad famine all through that country and he began to hurt. He signed on with a citizen there who assigned him to his fields to slop the pigs. He was so hungry he would have eaten the corncobs in the pig slop, but no one would give him any.

"That brought him to his senses. He said, 'All those farmhands working for my father sit down to three meals a day, and here I am starving to death. I'm going back to my father. I'll say to him, Father, I've sinned against God, I've sinned before you; I don't deserve to be called your son. Take me on as a hired hand.' He got right up and went home to his father.

"When he was still a long way off, his father saw him. His heart pounding, he ran out, embraced him, and kissed him. The son started his speech: 'Father, I've sinned against God, I've sinned before you; I don't deserve to be called your son ever again.'

"But the father wasn't listening. He was calling to the servants, 'Quick. Bring a clean set of clothes and dress him. Put the family ring on his finger and sandals on his feet. Then get a grain-fed heifer and roast it. We're going to feast! We're going to have a wonderful time! My son is here—given up for dead and now alive! Given up for lost and now found!' And they began to have a wonderful time.

"All this time his older son was out in the field. When the day's work was done he came in. As he approached the house, he heard the music and dancing. Calling over one of the houseboys, he asked what was going on. He told him, 'Your brother came home. Your father has ordered a feast—barbecued beef!—because he has him home safe and sound.'

"The older brother stalked off in an angry sulk and refused to join in. His father came out and tried to talk to him, but he wouldn't listen. The son said, 'Look how many years I've stayed here serving you, never giving you one moment of grief, but have you ever thrown a party for me and my friends? Then this son of yours who has thrown away your money on whores shows up and you go all out with a feast!'

"His father said, 'Son, you don't understand. You're with me all the time, and everything that is mine is yours — but this is a wonderful time, and we had to celebrate. This brother of yours was dead, and he's alive! He was lost, and he's found!'"

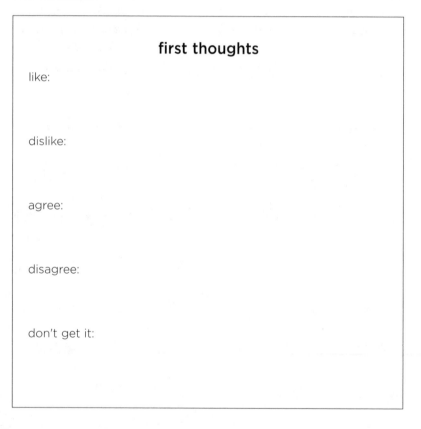

first thoughts

like:

dislike:

agree:

disagree:

don't get it:

think

- According to this story, how did each son's relationship with his father change? In what ways did the father's heart toward his sons change?
- In what ways has your relationship with your parents been changing over the last few years?
- Is there anything that makes it difficult for you to go home?
- Which of the sons in this story can you relate to more? Why?
- If this story were set in modern times, what would you say is the biggest miracle of the story?
- Which part of the story seems the most improbable in your life?

pray

live   The Redefining

Take a few moments to skim through the notes you've made in these readings. What do they tell you about your relationship with your parents? Based on what you've read and discussed, are there any changes you want to make in your relationship with them? Are there any issues you need to sit down and discuss?

What, if anything, is stopping you from making these changes or having this discussion with your parents?

Are you allowing anything to stop you from honoring your parents? If so, what is preventing you from fully honoring them? What changes do you need to make in your attitude, behavior, or actions?

Can you identify any unhealthy patterns in your relationship with your parents? If so, what can you do to break them?

Talk with a close friend about all of the above. Brainstorm together about what it might take to strengthen your relationship with your parents. Determine what this looks like in a practical sense and then list any measurable goals you want to shoot for here. Review these goals each week to see how you're doing.

learning to
live together

If you wake your friend in the early morning
by shouting "Rise and shine!"

It will sound to him
more like a curse than a blessing.

Proverbs 27:14

a reminder

Before you dive into this study, spend a little time reviewing what you wrote in the previous lessons' Live sections. How are you doing? Check with your small-group members and review your progress toward the specified goals. If necessary, adjust your goals and plans and then recommit to them.

the defining line

Learning to live with someone is one of life's greatest challenges. Whether in a college dorm, apartment complex, house, or other living situation, people who live under the same roof invariably have to learn to live together. If you're fortunate, you'll get to pick your roommates. But sometimes you won't. Whatever the circumstance, living with someone else reveals a lot more about you than it does the other person.

Living with another exposes personal strengths as well as shortcomings. You discover little things that drive you nuts as well as things that delight you.

And in the process, you learn what's truly important, not just around the house but also in the midst of human relationships.

Make a list of the different roommates you've had over the years. Place stars by your favorite roommates. What made them so enjoyable to live with? Circle your least favorite roommates. What made them such a challenge to live with? Now underline the roommates you treated the best. Do you see any correlations?

Reflecting on your list, write a want ad for the perfect roommate.

During the next small-group meeting, share your want ad with the group. Ask other members of your group to comment on what the ad reveals about you.

read The World of Roommates

From "Learning to Live with Your Roommate(s): Connections: These Are the People in Your Neighbourhood"[1]

Learning to live and get along with people you do not know very well can be one of the greatest challenges you will face. . . . Best friends often have the most difficult time living together, simply because they didn't sit down and talk about some ground rules for the year. You and your roommate(s) may become best friends, or you may not. You may choose to do very little together, or spend quite a bit of time together. Whichever way it works out for you, the experience will be equally valuable. It is through respecting one another's space and expressing your needs and wants that you will create the warm and open relationship that will contribute to a successful year. You will learn that each person is different, and what seems normal to you may be very foreign to your roommate(s). Your roommates are not the only people who will have pet peeves and strange habits; you will need to take a close look at yourself as well.

first thoughts

like:

dislike:

agree:

disagree:

don't get it:

think

- Why is "learning to live and get along with people" one of life's biggest challenges?
- What have your previous and/or current roommates revealed about your personality and disposition?
- What are the make-or-break issues that will either strengthen or undermine a roommate relationship?
- What does it take to live well with someone else? In what ways does living well with others reflect true Christianity?

pray

read A Dozen Roommates

Luke 6:12-16

At about that same time he climbed a mountain to pray. He was there all night in prayer before God. The next day he summoned his disciples; from them he selected twelve he designated as apostles:

Simon, whom he named Peter,
Andrew, his brother,
James,
John,
Philip,
Bartholomew,
Matthew,
Thomas,
James, son of Alphaeus,
Simon, called the Zealot,
Judas, son of James,
Judas Iscariot, who betrayed him.

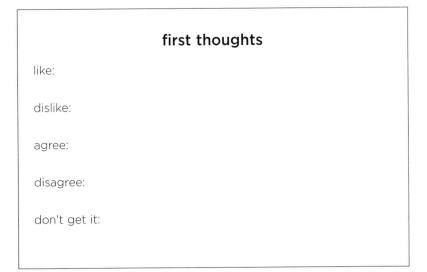

first thoughts

like:

dislike:

agree:

disagree:

don't get it:

think

- In what ways were Jesus' disciples a lot like roommates?
- Circle the names of the disciples you know the most about. Make a list of their personality traits, professions, and characteristics. Why do you think Jesus called such a diverse group of people?
- What challenges do you think the disciples faced in living, traveling, and ministering together?
- How do you think they grew through their experience of being together?

pray

read Frustration

Matthew 5:21-24

"You're familiar with the command to the ancients, 'Do not murder.' I'm telling you that anyone who is so much as angry with a brother or sister is guilty of murder. Carelessly call a brother 'idiot!' and you just might find yourself hauled into court. Thoughtlessly yell 'stupid!' at a sister and you are on the brink of hellfire. The simple moral fact is that words kill.

"This is how I want you to conduct yourself in these matters. If you enter your place of worship and, about to make an offering, you suddenly remember a grudge a friend has against you, abandon your offering, leave immediately, go to this friend and make things right. Then and only then, come back and work things out with God."

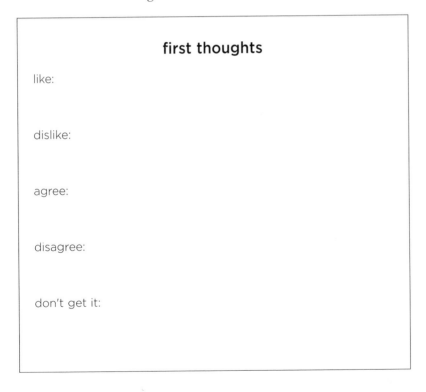

first thoughts

like:

dislike:

agree:

disagree:

don't get it:

think

- Why do you think it's so easy to get frustrated with room-mates?
- Are there any issues you've been putting off talking about with your roommates? What is stopping you from talking about them?
- Are there any issues for which you have not yet forgiven your roommates?
- What practical things can you do to be a better roommate?

pray

read When Things Explode

From "A Bruised Heart and a Beaten Couch" by LaTonya Taylor[2]

"How was your day?" my roommate asked as I trudged into our apartment.

I felt exhausted and sad, but I was glad she'd asked. I couldn't remember the last time I'd had a day this bad. I'd been struggling lately because a close friendship had ended. And although I'd really trusted this friend, he'd started acting in ways that felt confusing and mean.

I sat down on the couch and calmly told her about my day and the latest painful chapter of this rapidly-worsening story.

"You seem really calm," she said. A lot of people had told me that—that I seemed very calm and peaceful, that I was handling things so maturely and well, that it was OK if I felt hurt or upset. In fact, another friend had told me the same thing over dinner just a couple of hours before I came home.

The thing is, I wasn't pretending to be OK. I really thought that I was fine. *Friends come, and friends go*, I told myself. *You'll be OK.*

But as I told my roommate about my crummy day with this crummy friend, I felt my voice rising slightly with each sentence. My breathing became a little shallow, and my face was hot. I was crying again—but not the sad, heartbroken tears I'd been crying for the last few days. This was something new, something unfamiliar and intense.

My roommate watched me silently from across the living room as I stared at her in shock.

"I'm angry," I said, surprised as a host of feelings that had hidden behind a numb surface rose. "I'm so angry." Until that point, I'd had no idea just how bad I felt—how hurt and pained and full of pure rage this broken friendship had left me. I got up from the couch and rushed to my bedroom closet. Pulling on my hiking boots, I went back to the couch without even bothering to tie the laces.

"You hurt me!" I screamed at my now-former friend, kicking the couch so hard it moved a couple of inches toward the wall. "I trusted you, and you hurt me!" I wailed, half crying, half screaming as hot, salty tears streamed down my face, into my mouth, onto my shirt and the carpet below. For once,

I didn't bother to wipe them away. I just didn't care how I looked. I just didn't care. I cried and screamed as loud as I could, shrieking like the wounded person I was. I moaned and hiccuped and screamed at my bad friend, at myself for being his friend, at the whole world that I felt had treated me so unfairly.

For a good twenty minutes, I beat the couch with my fists. I kicked the arms of the couch and punched the back. I threw my body on it, sobbing and kicking like a child throwing a tantrum. I bawled and raged in ways I hadn't before then and I haven't since. Finally, I fell on the couch and sat there, sweaty, exhausted and spent. My caring roommate prayed aloud that God would heal my bruised spirit.

To be honest with you, I had no idea that I had so much rage and pain in my heart until it spilled out of me that day. And if you'd told me that I'd get it out by attacking furniture, I would have rolled my eyes at you. Even now, I wouldn't recommend tossing chairs around or slamming doors when you're upset.

But I also have to be honest and tell you that beating the couch was a very healing thing for me. The Bible warns us not to let our anger cause us to sin (Ephesians 4:26). I was deeply angry at my friend for the way he'd treated me. But beating up on my couch and screaming allowed me to get that anger out without saying ugly things to him or finding other ways to hurt him. So let me share with you what I learned: First, that it's OK to be angry when something bad happens. Many mental health professionals say that realizing you are angry can help you get on with your life and feelings after a painful incident.

The second thing I learned is that it's good to find a way that lets you get your anger out without hurting others—a healthy way, like journaling or going for a jog or, well, beating the couch (you should probably ask someone first, if you don't own the couch!). It's not good to keep painful feelings bottled up inside. That terrible outburst helped me to see how serious my feelings were, and how strong they were. I'm glad that I beat the couch and let them out. Keeping them inside would have been really self-destructive.

The third thing I learned? Let the friends and other loving people God's placed in your life take care of you. Friends like my roommate helped me get through the bad time I went through. They were reminders that no matter what I'm feeling, God is there. He's not afraid of my feelings, no matter how ugly or awful they seem to me.

first thoughts

like:

dislike:

agree:

disagree:

don't get it:

think

- Have you ever had a beating-the-couch experience? What triggered it?
- How do you deal with anger and pain in your life? Do you have a healthy outlet? If not, how can you replace your current anger outlet with one that is healthier?

- Can you think of a time when a broken friendship wounded your spirit? How did you recover? Are there any wounds that still need healing?
- What role are roommates responsible for playing when one of the people they're living with is hurting? What can be assumed? What can't?

pray

read Live Freely

Galatians 5:13-26

It is absolutely clear that God has called you to a free life. Just make sure that you don't use this freedom as an excuse to do whatever you want to do and destroy your freedom. Rather, use your freedom to serve one another in love; that's how freedom grows. For everything we know about God's Word is summed up in a single sentence: Love others as you love yourself. That's an act of true freedom. If you bite and ravage each other, watch out—in no time at all you will be annihilating each other, and where will your precious freedom be then?

My counsel is this: Live freely, animated and motivated by God's Spirit. Then you won't feed the compulsions of selfishness. For there is a root of sinful self-interest in us that is at odds with a free spirit, just as the free spirit is incompatible with selfishness. These two ways of life are antithetical, so that you cannot live at times one way and at times another way according to how you feel on any given day. Why don't you choose to be led by the Spirit and so escape the erratic compulsions of a law-dominated existence?

It is obvious what kind of life develops out of trying to get your own way all the time: repetitive, loveless, cheap sex; a stinking accumulation of mental and emotional garbage; frenzied and joyless grabs for happiness; trinket gods; magic-show religion; paranoid loneliness; cutthroat competition; all-consuming-yet-never-satisfied wants; a brutal temper; an impotence to love or be loved; divided homes and divided lives; small-minded and lopsided pursuits; the vicious habit of depersonalizing everyone into a rival; uncontrolled and uncontrollable addictions; ugly parodies of community. I could go on.

This isn't the first time I have warned you, you know. If you use your freedom this way, you will not inherit God's kingdom.

But what happens when we live God's way? He brings gifts into our lives, much the same way that fruit appears in an orchard—things like affection for others, exuberance about life, serenity. We develop a willingness to stick with things, a sense of compassion in the heart, and a conviction that a basic holiness permeates things and people. We find ourselves involved in loyal commitments, not needing to force our way in life, able to marshal and direct our energies wisely.

Legalism is helpless in bringing this about; it only gets in the way. Among those who belong to Christ, everything connected with getting our own way and mindlessly responding to what everyone else calls necessities is killed off for good—crucified.

Since this is the kind of life we have chosen, the life of the Spirit, let us make sure that we do not just hold it as an idea in our heads or a sentiment in our hearts, but work out its implications in every detail of our lives. That means we will not compare ourselves with each other as if one of us were better and another worse. We have far more interesting things to do with our lives. Each of us is an original.

---

first thoughts

like:

dislike:

agree:

disagree:

don't get it:

---

think

- Underline the statements that you resonate with in this passage. Which of them have you seen play out in your relationships with your roommates?
- What are some things you have to give up in order to be a good roommate?
- What situations tend to bring out your selfishness?
- In what areas of your life and faith are you tempted to be legalistic? In what areas do you need to become more understanding toward others?
- In what ways does living with someone day in and day out provide a laboratory for learning about yourself and the way you function in relationships?

pray

live   The Redefining

Take a few moments to skim through the notes you've made in these readings. What do they tell you about your defining characteristics? Based on what you've read and discussed, are there any areas in your life that you need to change?

What, if anything, is stopping you from making these changes?

What can you do to become a "roommate" not just to the people who live in your building but to those who live in the same community as you?

Are there any areas in which you need to grow in compassion, forgiveness, or grace? If so, describe them.

Talk with a close friend about all of the above. Brainstorm together about what it might take to move toward God in this area of your life. Determine what this looks like in a practical sense and then list any measurable goals you want to shoot for here. Review these goals each week to see how you're doing.

we're so
different

God's various gifts are handed out everywhere; but they all originate in God's Spirit. God's various ministries are carried out everywhere; but they all originate in God's Spirit. God's various expressions of power are in action everywhere; but God himself is behind it all. Each person is given something to do that shows who God is: Everyone gets in on it, everyone benefits. All kinds of things are handed out by the Spirit, and to all kinds of people! . . . All these gifts have a common origin, but are handed out one by one by the one Spirit of God. He decides who gets what, and when.

1 Corinthians 12:4-7,11

a reminder
Before you dive into this study, spend a little time reviewing what you wrote in the previous lessons' Live sections. How are you doing? Check with your small-group members and review your progress toward the specified goals. If necessary, adjust your goals and plans and then recommit to them.

the defining line
Dealing with diversity isn't always easy, but it's always good. Being around people who are different from you—whether in personality, background, or

even faith—helps you expand your understanding of yourself and the world around you. It challenges your attitudes, beliefs, and behaviors and helps you become more like Christ.

Make a list of three friends you would consider opposites of you.

What makes them so different from you? What draws you toward them?

What are some of the interpersonal challenges that naturally arise in these relationships? How do you deal with them? How could you deal with them more effectively?

Consider sharing your responses with your group when you meet.

read The Conflict of Diversity

From "The Downside of Diversity" by Angela Pirisi[1]

More and more companies are asking employees to leave the isolation of their cubicles to collaborate with coworkers, spawning innovative ideas, increased productivity—and, surprisingly, friction.

According to Debra Connelley, Ph.D., who teaches organizational behavior at the University of Buffalo, increasing diversity and team-based work structures can spark office conflict. This is typical, she says, of any environment in which very different types of people are forced to interact closely while attempting to assert their own goals and personal values.

Ethnicity, religion and gender are just a few of the major factors that lead people to clash over opposing viewpoints. Even one's work or education background can influence one's personal perspective. People tend to shut out information that doesn't mesh with their own beliefs, especially when it comes from someone they don't like or trust, says Connelley. Moreover, people define problems differently and attribute the causes to different sources.

But employers can watch for warning signs that conflict is mounting: Arguments arise regularly during meetings; a work team fails to reach a consensus; team productivity wanes in comparison to individual output; or employees make themselves unavailable for group meetings by taking a sick day or booking appointments during those times.

Bosses can boost poor group morale by training employees in conflict management as well as by emphasizing the importance of communication with coworkers. Most importantly, employees

---

first thoughts

like:

dislike:

agree:

disagree:

don't get it:

must learn to be flexible. Says Connelley: "People have to learn to respond to others' perspectives not with a kneejerk reaction but by waiting to hear out information before they make a decision."

think

- What do you think about Connelley's final statement in the article? On a practical level, is this easy or hard to do? Why?
- In what ways have you seen "ethnicity, religion and gender" issues create conflict?
- Do you think the innovation produced by diversity is worth the cost of conflict? Why or why not?
- In what ways is a person forced to grow when he or she is exposed to new people and ideas? Is it possible to refuse to grow?
- What can you do to maximize personal growth when there is diversity in your life?

pray

read Dealing with Difficult People

From "Okay, What *About* Bob?" by Margaret Feinberg[2]

Anyone who is actively involved in Christian ministry knows that it's only a matter of time until God sends you Bob. Who is Bob? In the everyday world, a "Bob" is the "odd man out." Bob can come in the form of Bobbie depending on the gender (and please note that this is a slang term, not to be confused with people named Robert, Roberta or otherwise). In our fellowships, I'd like to describe Bob as 1) a person sent by God to challenge and test your leadership skills; 2) a member of the body of Christ who doesn't fit in the way we expect; 3) a Christian who promptly brings you to your knees to pray, "How do we care for this one?" and 4) one of God's special people.

I encountered my first Bob while leading a series of college prayer meetings. Though Bob was several years older than everyone else in the group, he attended faithfully every week. He always came a few minutes early and had a tendency to be one of the last to leave. Bob always offered lengthy prayers which included Scripture recited from memory detailing the chapter and verse. Bob's prayers were basically the same each week. It seemed a bit odd that he never mentioned anything about his personal life. While the other members of the prayer group shared heartfelt needs and were growing closer to each other, Bob stayed on the fringe.

Within a few months, Bob seemed to become more of a burden than a blessing. He made unnecessary comments. His prayers never changed. He said annoying and inappropriate things. His jokes weren't funny. He even had bad breath. Sadly, it was a relief when Bob missed a meeting. It became

---

first thoughts

like:

dislike:

agree:

disagree:

don't get it:

---

apparent that Bob didn't fit into the culture of our prayer group except for one factor: he loved Jesus Christ. And that made him part of the body of Christ—whether we liked it or not.

think

- Has God ever placed a Bob in your life? How did you react or respond?
- What is your natural tendency toward Bob-like people? What prevents you from being more Christlike toward the Bobs of the world?
- In what ways are you a Bob? Do you think everyone has at least one Bob-like characteristic? Why or why not?

pray

read Sinners for Dinner

Luke 15:1-10

By this time a lot of men and women of doubtful reputation were hanging around Jesus, listening intently. The Pharisees and religion scholars were not pleased, not at all pleased. They growled, "He takes in sinners and eats meals with them, treating them like old friends." Their grumbling triggered this story.

"Suppose one of you had a hundred sheep and lost one. Wouldn't you leave the ninety-nine in the wilderness and go after the lost one until you found it? When found, you can be sure you would put it across your shoulders, rejoicing, and when you got home call in your friends and neighbors, saying, 'Celebrate with me! I've found my lost sheep!' Count on it—there's more joy in heaven over one sinner's rescued life than over ninety-nine good people in no need of rescue.

"Or imagine a woman who has ten coins and loses one. Won't she light a lamp and scour the house, looking in every nook and cranny until she finds it? And when she finds it you can be sure she'll call her friends and neighbors: 'Celebrate with me! I found my lost coin!' Count on it—that's the kind of party God's angels throw every time one lost soul turns to God."

first thoughts

like:

dislike:

agree:

disagree:

don't get it:

think

- Why do you think Jesus used stories to respond to the situation with the unhappy Pharisees and scholars? What was He trying to communicate?
- In what ways is God calling you to search for a lost "sheep" or "coin"?
- Is it ever inappropriate or unhealthy to spend time with people of "doubtful reputation"? Are there situations in which you need to take a step back from those types of relationships? If so, explain.
- What does this story say about judging by appearances? Can you think of any situations recently when you have been tempted to do so?

pray

read Breaking Down the Marriage Barrier

From "Extended Family Values: Why Married and Single Families Need Each Other" by Andy Crouch[3]

Christian community made my own years as an unmarried person very rich—so rich that marriage snuck up on me. I lived for four years in a household on Mount Auburn Street in the heart of Cambridge's Harvard Square. Depending on the year, four to six post-college twentysomethings ate together, prayed together, and entertained friends together. For several years, the members of the household shared one bank account, which soared and dipped dramatically along with our career fortunes. Guided by a covenant that we reaffirmed each year, we sought to live out Luke's description of the early church, the one so often quoted and so little practiced: "All who believed were together and had all things in common; they would sell their possessions and goods and distribute the proceeds to all, as any had need." (Quite true—one year Steve lost his job and spent the next nine months unemployed, on us.) "Day by day, as they spent much time together in the temple" (historical circumstances prevented us from doing that part), "they broke bread at home and ate their food with glad and generous hearts" (creative amateur chefs are integral to the success of any Christian community, and ours was no exception), "praising God and having the goodwill of all the people." (I don't know what all the people thought of us, but our neighbors liked us well enough.) "And the Lord added to their number daily those who were being saved." (Not daily. But regularly.)

It is possible to be lonely anywhere, of course. But in that household I could go for weeks with only a vague awareness of my aloneness. My life, in its mundane and profound aspects, was full. Christian community is a powerful antidote to loneliness.

In the fourth year of living on Mount Auburn Street, however, I found myself, as Walter Wangerin memorably describes, "pitched headlong into a crisis wherein I suffered a blindness, from which I arose—married." In God's inscrutable providence, so did two other men from my household. In the course of a summer, like some highly unstable molecule, our community had split into three marriages and two free radicals.

It is at this point—the beginning of marriage and family—that most North Americans begin the long retreat into the nuclear isolation so celebrated by proponents of "family values." Experiments like the household at Mount Auburn Street may be tolerable, even enviable, holding patterns for single persons, but once those persons marry, powerful internal and external forces discourage them from pursuing more lasting forms of day-in, day-out relationship with other Christians. Housing, especially outside of urban areas, is constructed to serve the nuclear family. The real needs of a marriage for privacy—and the false needs conjured up by our atomized American conception of liberty—make any sort of "extended family" seem unrealistic at best, suffocating at worst. Sharing living space seems like an impossible intrusion to people who balk at sharing a lawnmower.

Even at the simpler level of friendship, married persons quickly find themselves socializing primarily with other couples. Churches provide a lifetime's worth of fellowship opportunities that trade on marital status—the young marrieds' Sunday School class, the parents' club, and so forth. With so many opportunities, small wonder that some newlyweds behave like former slum residents who have hit the lottery jackpot—moving out and leaving their single friends behind. Is it any wonder that singles are obsessed with getting married or, at least, finding a companion?

Here, again, the biblical world offers something different. The early Christians lived in a world, not of nuclear families, but "households." These complex assemblies of an extended family, slaves, freedmen, business associates, and tenants were the basic building block of Greco-Roman society. And when the gospel touched people's lives, it touched their households. Priscilla and Aquila, Philemon, and Stephanos all opened their homes to the Christian community. Paul wrote his letters largely to "household churches," which shared many of the characteristics of actual households, from regular meals to the holy kiss of affection. The ubiquitous Pauline forms of address, "brothers" or "beloved," underlined what Paul made explicit in his letters: we are all part of the "household of God" (Ephesians 2:19), which is not so much a cozy Trinity-plus-two-kids arrangement as a multifaceted extended family from all walks of life.

What would it mean to recapture this sort of household church today? This has been a driving question in my own marriage since Catherine and I committed, during our engagement, to resist the cultural forces that would tend to isolate us from our still-single friends. Our pre-marriage experiences with community and the convictions that were formed there have led us, in each year of our marriage, into a household with others—our first year, with one other single person, and for the past several years, with another married couple and two single persons. We are not alone in extending our family in this way—we count among our friends several similar households in Boston, as well as in California, Mississippi, Wisconsin, and elsewhere. Though their form varies, these households all have something in common: married couples, children, and single people making a common life of prayer, fellowship, and ministry in one home. This common life brings gifts and challenges. (Usually the gifts are the challenges.) In particular, life in a household has everything to do with making both singleness and marriage into true and livable Christian callings.

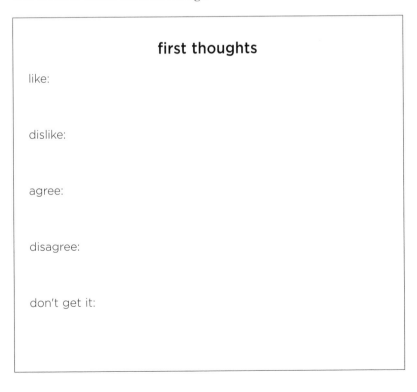

first thoughts

like:

dislike:

agree:

disagree:

don't get it:

think

- How many of your friends have gotten married? How have those marriages affected your friendships?
- What are some of the challenges couples and singles face when trying to maintain friendships? Why do you think singles tend to hang out with other singles and couples with other couples?
- Can you think of people who are an exception to this tendency? What makes them different in their attitudes and actions?
- How are you personally enriched by hanging out with people from a different marital status? How is the body of Christ strengthened when married people and single people grow side by side in authentic community?

pray

read Getting Over Yourself

From "I Hate Stupid People" by J. R. Rushik[4]

"I hate stupid people." I smiled the first time I read that bumper sticker. Finally, someone understood. That sticker gave me permission to label anyone who wasn't like me as "stupid." And boy did I meet a lot of stupid people. Stupid people began to show up all around me. They were in front of me on the highway. We shared a seat on a plane ride. They were around me at amusement parks, at the beach, in the mall. Stupid people seemed to be reproducing everywhere. Who were they and where did they come from? How could this world become so littered with stupid people?

It's easy to hate people. It gives you something to talk about. It provides a platform on which to elevate yourself. People who hate people are actually saying, "I expect the world to revolve around me. Period."

One day I realized my attitude had to change. So I began a quest to really love and appreciate people. And I found every person is unique and of great value. It was easy to appreciate people who are like me, people of similar tastes, talents and tendencies. The more difficult task was learning to love people who are very different than me. In order to grow in this area, I had to move out of my comfort zones.

Below are three simple experiences that helped me to gain a deeper appreciation for the diversity found in people. I challenge you to branch out in some of these areas and dive into the current of a world outside of your comfort zones.

[I TOOK THE BUS]

I sat in the back of a bus that was traveling through a poor area of town. My goal was to merely watch and learn from those around me. I saw a man who looked like he'd lost the game of life. He was beaten, worn out and tired. However, my stereotypes were shattered when he tipped his hat for every lady entering the bus and eventually gave up his seat to another tired soul. Many people caught that bus during the 52 minutes I was in the back, and each one was teeming with their own brand of life. I realized every person is writing their own "living story" and I could learn a lot from them.

Lesson #1 Observe and appreciate the value of people who are different than yourself.

[I TOOK THE SMALL PIECE]

It was Krista's birthday and I grabbed the last piece of cake. I went back to my table and saw Kevin didn't get any cake. So, I cut the cake in two and offered half to Kevin. Kevin reached out and took the smaller piece of cake. I said, "Kev, you took the small piece." He said, "JR, I always take the small piece. It illustrates that you care more about the other person than you do for yourself." So next time I had the opportunity, I took the small piece. I'm not sure if anyone noticed, but something began to change inside of me. My eyes were opened to the reality that other people's needs are just as important as mine.

Lesson #2 Put other people's needs before your own.

[I TOLD THEIR STORY]

As the clouds began to lift in my life and my focus shifted from the "me-god" to the beauty of other people, my conversations began to change. Instead of downgrading other people (in an attempt to elevate myself), I found delight in sharing the stories of others. In fact, with each story I got more and more excited to observe, learn and serve more people. By shifting the focus from "me" to "them" my life was radically changed.

Lesson #3 Share with others the good things you see in those around you.

Three actions, observe, serve and share, changed in my life. They moved me down a road toward truly loving and valuing the diversity of people all around.

I'm still working on each of these three elements on a daily basis. I know when I get them right I'll begin to catch a glimpse of how God views each of us every day. And all those "stupid people" labels will continue to fall off at an increased rate. And I realize just how valuable every person truly is.

---

first thoughts

like:

dislike:

agree:

disagree:

don't get it:

---

think

- Why is it so easy to "hate stupid people"? In what ways are you tempted to give in to this tendency?
- When was the last time you found yourself hating others like the writer describes? What was the situation? What triggered it? How did you get past it?
- In addition to what the author listed, what practical things can you do to avoid getting frustrated with others?

pray

live   The Redefining

Take a few moments to skim through the notes you've made in these readings. What do they tell you about how you deal with people who are different from you? Based on what you've read and discussed, is there anything you want to change?

What, if anything, is stopping you from making this change?

Do you have any attitudes or prejudices that you need to confront? Do you sense God asking you to be more understanding, gracious, or kind to any individuals or groups of people?

In what ways do your relationships reflect Christ being lived out in real time?

Talk with a close friend about all of the above. Brainstorm together about what it might take to move toward God in this area of your life. Determine what this looks like in a practical sense and then list any measurable goals you want to shoot for here. Review these goals each week to see how you're doing.

challenges of male-female relationships

In Christ's family there can be no division into
Jew and non-Jew, slave and free, male and female.
Among us you are all equal. That is, we are all
in a common relationship with Jesus Christ.

Galatians 3:28

a reminder

*Before you dive into this study, spend a little time reviewing what
you wrote in the previous lessons' Live sections. How are you doing?
Check with your small-group members and review your progress
toward the specified goals. If necessary, adjust your goals and plans
and then recommit to them.*

the defining line

It's no secret that men and women sometimes struggle to keep their relationships on a friendship level. Some would say that the more time you
spend and the more activities you do together, the tougher it gets not to
become emotionally involved. In what ways do you agree with this? In what
ways do you disagree?

Have you ever been involved in a friendship with someone of the opposite sex and woken up one day thinking, *I want this to be something more?* What did you do with those feelings? What do you think is the best way to handle those feelings? How does the response differ depending on the situation?

Do you think it's possible for men and women to maintain healthy, nonromantic relationships? Why or why not?

Consider sharing your responses with your group when you meet.

read On Friendships

From "Can Men and Women Be Friends?" by Camille Chatterjee[1]

Researchers tell us that men and women can be friends. But do we really believe them? A survey of more than 1,450 members of the match.com dating site revealed that we're an optimistic bunch:

1. Do you believe men and women can be platonic friends?

    Yes: 83%
    No: 11%
    Unsure: 6%

2. Have you had a platonic friendship that crossed the line and became romantic or sexual?

    Yes: 62%
    No: 36%
    Unsure: 2%

3. Who is more likely to misinterpret the intimacy of friendship for sexual desire?

    Men: 64%
    Women: 25%
    Unsure: 11%

4. Is it possible to fall in love with someone who first enters your life as a friend?

    Yes: 94%
    No: 4%
    Unsure: 2%

5. Do you hope that when you do fall in love, your partner will have started out as your friend?

> Yes: 71%
> No: 9%
> Unsure: 20%

6. Who is better at keeping sex out of a platonic relationship?

> Men: 13%
> Women: 67%
> Unsure: 20%

---

first thoughts

like:

dislike:

agree:

disagree:

don't get it:

---

think

- Do any of the answers in this survey surprise you? Are any of the percentages higher or lower than you expected? Explain.
- If this survey were taken by Christians only, how might the responses be different? For which questions do you think the responses would be the same?
- Can you think of any personal relationships in which you discovered these statistics to be true? If so, describe the situation.
- Why do you think men and women sometimes struggle to be "just friends"?

pray

read The Nonromantic Relationship

From "Can Platonic Relationships Really Exist?" by Erica Williams[2]

When dealing with male-female relationships, the statement of "we're just friends," is frequently followed by snickers of doubt and "yeah, right" attitudes. But why is this? Lisa Bradshaw, a counselor at George Mason University, says the prevalent belief is that it is simply impossible for males and females to just be friends.

"Wherever a friendship between two people of the opposite sex is seen, society makes predictions about how the friendship is doomed to fail because intimate feelings will usually get involved," said Bradshaw.

The general view is that sooner or later, the relationship will get too intimate for comfort. According to Hindu Mish, a doctor and counselor at George Mason University, this view has been paralleled in numerous urban colleges across the United States.

However, as times change, so do people. The social scene is undergoing a slight change that is more accepting of platonic relationships. Boys and girls are getting to know each other without the context of one-on-one relationships. Group dating is increasing, enabling people to forge strong, non-sexual, respectable relationships with one another.

This changing scenario proves that people are capable of forming lasting relationships with members of the opposite sex. Relations between the two genders increasingly rely on respect and friendship rather than just sex and/or intimacy.

Although platonic relationships exist, there is always the possibility that the relationship will evolve into something more. But relationships that begin with friendship as their base have been proven to be far more stable than those that do not.

"Relationships that have friendship as their base usually last longer because both partners are more comfortable around each other," Dr. Hindu said. "There are no pretensions in the relationship. This, along with other factors, proves that even if male/female friendships escalate, they can still be healthy relationships."

The views of platonic relationships differ in various people. Although many platonic relationships have been proven healthy, many people feel as if a man and a woman cannot be friends without being intimate.

Although platonic relationships do exist and can actually work, these relationships may require more work than same-sex friendships. Although it is important to cultivate all friendships, be mindful of hazards that might jeopardize a platonic relationship.

In order for the friendship to work, you must be up front about your feelings. Counselors suggest that if romantic sentiments arise, it is easier to reveal those feelings at the start of the friendship. Mixed emotions can get in the way later on if you feel very passionate about developing a committed relationship with your platonic friend.

On the other hand, if you are only interested in a platonic relationship and feel you can maintain it, then go for it! With this attitude in mind, it's very possible that a platonic relationship can work. If a mutual understanding exists and both parties agree to the status of their relationship, the friendship can stand the test of time.

first thoughts

like:

dislike:

agree:

disagree:

don't get it:

think

- Why do you think platonic (nonromantic) relationships are difficult to maintain? Do you think some people are better at maintaining platonic relationships than others? If so, what are some of the qualities or characteristics of people who are better able to maintain them?
- What are some of the most common hazards that can jeopardize a platonic relationship? How do you balance getting close to someone without getting too close?
- Do you think this generation is more prone to group dates? Why or why not? Would you prefer a group date or a one-on-one date with someone you're getting to know? Why?

pray

read Is Friendship Possible?

From "Can Men and Women Be Friends?" by Camille Chatterjee[3]

If men are from Mars and women are from Venus, it may explain at least one of their shared beliefs: Men and women can't be real friends. Blame the sexual tension that almost inevitably exists between any red-blooded, heterosexual man and woman. Point to the jealousy that plagues many rational people when a significant other befriends someone of the opposite sex. Boil it down to the inherent differences between the sexes.

It just can't be done. Right?

Wrong, say relationship experts. "The belief that men and women can't be friends comes from another era in which women were at home and men were in the workplace, and the only way they could get together was for romance," explains Linda Sapadin, Ph.D., a psychologist in private practice in Valley Stream, New York. "Now they work together and have sports interests together and socialize together." This cultural shift is encouraging psychologists, sociologists and communications experts to put forth a new message: Though it may be tricky, men and women can successfully become close friends. What's more, there are good reasons for them to do so.

Society has long singled out romance as the prototypical male-female relationship because it spawns babies and keeps the life cycle going; cross-sex friendship, as researchers call it, has been either ignored or trivialized. We have rules for how to act in romantic relationships (flirt, date, get married, have kids) and even same-sex friendships (boys relate by doing activities together, girls by talking and sharing). But there are so few platonic male-female friendships on display in our culture that we're at a loss to even define these relationships.

Part of this confusion stems from the media. A certain 1989 film starring Meg Ryan and Billy Crystal convinced a nation of moviegoers that sex always comes between men and women, making true friendship impossible. "*When Harry Met Sally* set the potential for male-female friendship back about 25 years," says Michael Monsour, Ph.D., assistant professor of communications at the University of Colorado at Denver and author of *Women and Men as Friends: Relationships Across the Life Span in the 21st Century* (Lawrence Erlbaum,

2001). Television hasn't helped either. "Almost every time you see a male-female friendship, it winds up turning into romance," Monsour notes. Think Sam and Diane or Chandler and Monica. These cultural images are hard to overcome, he says. It's no wonder we expect that men and women are always on the road to romance.

But that's only one of the major barriers. In 1989, Don O'Meara, Ph.D., a sociology professor at the University of Cincinnati-Raymond Walters College, published a landmark study in the journal *Sex Roles* on the top impediments to cross-sex friendship. "I started my research because one of my best friends is a woman," says O'Meara. "She said, 'Do you think anyone else has the incredible friendship we do?'" He decided to find out, and after reviewing the scant existing research dating back to only 1974, O'Meara identified the following four challenges to male-female friendship: defining it, dealing with sexual attraction, seeing each other as equals and facing people's responses to the relationship. A few years later, he added a fifth: meeting in the first place.

first thoughts

like:

dislike:

agree:

disagree:

don't get it:

think

- Do you think it's important for men and women to develop healthy bonds of friendship? What kinds of benefits have you experienced from this type of friendship in your own life?
- Why do male-female relationships often become "weird" or "awkward"? From your own experience, what can be done to build and protect a healthy male-female friendship?
- Underline the challenges O'Meara identified in his study of male-female friendships. Which can you identify with? Which would you say is the most challenging? Least challenging? Why?

pray

read Preserving Friendships

1 John 2:1-11

I write this, dear children, to guide you out of sin. But if anyone does sin, we have a Priest-Friend in the presence of the Father: Jesus Christ, righteous Jesus. When he served as a sacrifice for our sins, he solved the sin problem for good—not only ours, but the whole world's.

Here's how we can be sure that we know God in the right way: Keep his commandments.

If someone claims, "I know him well!" but doesn't keep his commandments, he's obviously a liar. His life doesn't match his words. But the one who keeps God's word is the person in whom we see God's mature love. This is the only way to be sure we're in God. Anyone who claims to be intimate with God ought to live the same kind of life Jesus lived.

My dear friends, I'm not writing anything new here. This is the oldest commandment in the book, and you've known it from day one. It's always been implicit in the Message you've heard. On the other hand, perhaps it is new, freshly minted as it is in both Christ and you—the darkness on its way out and the True Light already blazing!

Anyone who claims to live in God's light and hates a brother or sister is still in the dark. It's the person who loves brother and sister who dwells in God's light and doesn't block the light from others. But whoever hates is still in the dark, stumbles around in the dark, doesn't know which end is up, blinded by the darkness.

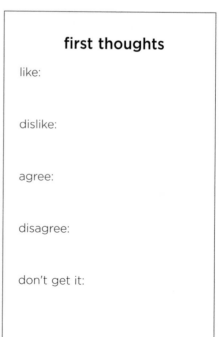

first thoughts

like:

dislike:

agree:

disagree:

don't get it:

think

- What is "the oldest commandment in the book"? Why is it so crucial for preserving friendships?
- What can you do to keep your friendships with people of the opposite sex in the "True Light"? What can you do to reconcile relationships when mistakes are made?
- How can you keep God's commandments in your relationships?

pray

read Gender Benders

From *How to Be a Grown-Up: 247 Lab-Tested Strategies for Conquering the World* by Margaret Feinberg and Leif Oines[4]

He Said, She Heard

Ever feel like you're not getting through? Like you're saying one thing, and the gal is hearing something completely different? Here's a short guide for those kinds of moments:

He Said	She Heard
"Wanna grab dinner?"	"What should we name our first child?"
"Nothing's wrong . . . why?"	"I don't feel comfortable enough to share my intimate thoughts with you."
"I'm going out with the guys."	"You aren't fun enough or cool enough to meet my needs."
"You look great in that dress!"	"Every other dress you've ever worn makes you look fat."
"Let's just be friends."	"I hate you!"

She Said, He Heard

Not communicating well goes both ways. You say one thing, and the guy hears something completely different. Here's a short guide for those kinds of moments:

She Said	He Heard
"I love you like a brother."	"I hereby reject your manhood with six words."
"Nothing's wrong!"	"Nothing is wrong. Everything's great. Let's watch football."
"Does my butt look big in these?"	"Danger! Danger! You can't win! Don't answer this! Run away!"
"Fine! Go out with your friends!"	"It's okay, honey. Have a great time. I'll be right here whenever you're ready. Maybe I'll bake a pie."
"So where do you see this going?"	"Just exactly when are you going to commit, buy a ring, talk to my dad, walk down the aisle, and give up your freedom?"

first thoughts

like:

dislike:

agree:

disagree:

don't get it:

think

- Through humor, this passage illustrates some different communication styles among men and women. How do men and women communicate differently? How does this lead to miscommunication?
- In what situations are you most tempted to read into what someone says? How can this complicate a friendship with someone of the opposite sex?
- When you encounter a potential miscommunication, what is the best way to handle it? What prevents you from addressing miscommunication in this way?
- What can you do to maintain better communication with friends of the opposite sex?

pray

live   The Redefining

Take a few moments to skim through the notes you've made in these readings. What do they tell you about your friendships with people of the opposite sex? Do you think you have healthy or unhealthy relationships? Based on what you've read and discussed, is there anything you want to change?

What, if anything, is stopping you from making this change?

Do you think you have a healthy balance of male and female relationships in your life? Why or why not? What steps can you take to have a healthy balance?

How can you be a better friend to people of the opposite sex? Is there any behavior you need to change? Are there any unhealthy emotional or physical needs you're hoping will be filled?

What can you do to make the most of your friendships?

Talk with a close friend about all of the above. Brainstorm together about what it might take to move toward God in this area of your life. Determine what this looks like in a practical sense and then list any measurable goals you want to shoot for here. Review these goals each week to see how you're doing.

beyond
friends

Therefore a man leaves his father and mother and embraces his wife. They become one flesh.
The two of them, the Man and his Wife, were naked, but they felt no shame.

Genesis 2:24-25

a reminder

Before you dive into this study, spend a little time reviewing what you wrote in the previous lessons' Live sections. How are you doing? Check with your small-group members and review your progress toward the specified goals. If necessary, adjust your goals and plans and then recommit to them.

the defining line

In some ways it seems as though Adam and Eve had it pretty easy: one man and one woman. Without any options, the selection process for choosing a mate was simple. But in the modern world, the process of finding a spouse is much more complex. Relationship experts tout different formulas for finding love, such as dating and courting. Yet there doesn't seem to be a one-size-fits-all method. Why do you think there are so many ways people find true love?

When you think about the terms *dating*, *courting*, and *committed relationship*, what comes to mind? What are the differences among them? Why do you think so many people have different understandings of these terms?

Where did your understanding of these terms come from? How has your upbringing and personal experience influenced your understanding? How has Scripture and studying the Bible affected the way you think about them?

Consider sharing your responses with your group when you meet.

read Experiments in Dating

From "The Six-Month Dating Experiment: Part Two: Addressing My Neuroses" by Carla Jean Whitley[1]

When I made my New Year's resolutions, I didn't expect them to unfold as they have.

I'm not given to setting grandiose goals just because the calendar changes. But as I searched for a new planner and adjusted to writing 2005 on checks, I realized I needed more than these external changes. I needed to adjust my attitude toward men.

I don't have any tragic reasons for being the way I am (scared, bitter, overly analytical, stand-offish). But after a series of completely normal rejections and breakups, I gave up on maintaining healthy relationships with men. I built walls to keep my heart safe, and in the process my social skills regressed to those of a seventh grader. At least, that's the way it feels. Two weeks with Dr. Henry Cloud as my "dating coach" (via his book *How to Get a Date Worth Keeping: Be Dating in Six Months or Your Money Back*) have revealed just how far I have to go.

I asked a group of friends to hold me accountable during this six-month experiment. Not only do I want to be sure I am not doing anything unbiblical, I also want them to hold me to this commitment and tell me if they think I'm getting too serious too quickly. (Though at the moment it's hard to imagine even *one* date, much less a relationship!)

Then came step one. It sounded easy enough: I was to maintain a log of guys I met who fit three qualifications. They had to be new to me, have enough interaction with me to be interested and have a way to follow through. No action just yet—merely observation.

I wasn't surprised that I only logged one guy each of these two weeks. Neither was it a shock to see how many people I *could* be talking to—at church, at the library and even occasionally at work. My only surprise was how I reacted when they came around. My interaction with a man at work perfectly illustrates my problem. I met this attractive man one day—I even spent 20 minutes sitting by him at lunch. I could have counted the words I uttered on my fingers. I clammed up, afraid of saying something stupid or, worse still, looking like I was hitting on him. After he left, I realized how foolish I was. There were several safe questions I could have asked, just to get conversation rolling. "How long have you been working here?" "Where did you go to college?" "Where did you grow up?" They're nothing exciting, but at least I could have breached the awkward silence and gotten out of my head for a moment.

That's really the purpose of this experiment. I'm not on a mission to find free Friday night dinners or even a husband. My goal is to get past this paranoia I have around men and learn to enjoy friendships with them again. As Dr. Cloud wrote, "This book is about growing and healing your whole relational life, and as a result, your dating life will grow. Heal the tree, and the fruit will change."

It may take the full six months, but at least I'm on my way to transformation.

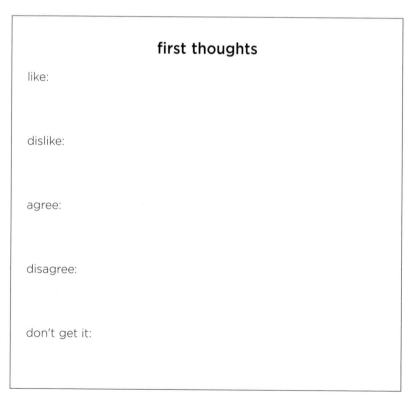

first thoughts

like:

dislike:

agree:

disagree:

don't get it:

think

- What aspects of dating come easily to you? What aspects are more difficult?
- Which of your insecurities tend to manifest themselves when you're talking to someone of the opposite sex or out on a date?
- Have you ever "clammed up" around someone? What caused it? How can you move beyond it?

pray

read Searching for "the One"

From the *CNN* report "Ready, Set, Date! HurryDate Offers Prospect of Romance in Four Minutes Flat"[2]

On the sound of a whistle, the singles scurry about the trendy bar before sitting down opposite a potential suitor.

They then chat, stare, smirk, joke, sigh—most anything, really, as long they do it in four minutes, when the whistle shrieks marking the end of one "date" and the start of another.

At HurryDate, this breakneck, dizzying approach to relationship building aims to generate long-lasting partnerships, one-night flings or, if nothing else, a few amusing anecdotes.

HurryDate is among several companies that try to curry relationships through parties, short and fast "dates" and the Internet. While matchmaking has been around for centuries, these ventures shoot to make romance easier in an era when time and access to other singles can be elusive.

"People are all over the place, and they don't have time to meet people," said Ken Deckinger, who founded HurryDate with longtime friend Adele Testani.

In the less than four years since its inception, the upstart company has hosted more than 2 million mini-dates involving thousands of singles. Today, HurryDate hosts 150 date "parties" a month held in 65 cities in the United States (in 28 states plus Washington, D.C.), the United Kingdom and Canada.

HurryDate's founders say they find as much satisfaction in building strong relationships as a strong business, claiming the company has fostered at least 83 engagements or marriages.

"There is something so rewarding about knowing that you are having a major impact on people's lives," said Deckinger, the company's CEO. "You're creating generations of people that are getting together and having families. It gives us chills."

Of course, not every short-lived date—at HurryDate or rival speed-dating companies—leads to a lifetime of wedded bliss.

Such microwave relationships hardly offer much time for soul searching, its co-founders concede. In a sense, quality may be sacrificed for quantity — a blessing, some may argue, compared to enduring a dreadful four-hour long blind date.

"We always say, you're not going to know if you want to marry a person in four minutes," said Testani, HurryDate's president. "It's really just to get a sense of rapport."

Such chemistry drew Testani and Deckinger together back when they first met, at age 15, during a scuba diving trip in their hometown of Boca Raton, Florida. (For the record, they say they never have and never plan to date one another.)

After attending rival high schools, the two went to the University of Florida in Gainesville before heading about 1,000 miles north to New York City.

There, Testani and Deckinger meshed their affinity for matchmaking and throwing parties by forming HurryDate, launching the company in May 2001.

By September 2001, the company reached about 10 cities, with new locations and ideas being added every month. Today, HurryDate offers assorted theme "parties" — depending on age, sexual preference, religion and other categories, like political affiliation during the recent presidential campaign — to match-up eager and available singles.

Creating an environment that allows singles to meet many people in a short period of time is nothing new, nor original to HurryDate. Numerous companies around the world — such as FastDater, 8minuteDating, 25Dates. com, TurboDate, among many others — work off the same basic concept.

Testani said HurryDate holds regular brainstorming sessions, to improve its business model and keep its parties fun, hip and fresh.

"The key to moving HurryDate forward is involving everyone, fresh ideas, creativity and be willing to take a risk," she said. "The dating world is a very competitive business, and it keeps you on your toes."

HurryDate's "parties" are structured to be enjoyable, fairly pressure-free and filled with singles looking for companionship, Testani said.

"You don't need to get up the nerve to talk to them — they're available and you'll be able to meet them," said Testani. "And getting to meet someone face-to-face is just so important, because that's where the chemistry happens."

After four-minute sessions, HurryDate participants—each with an identification number—mark "yes" or "no" as to whether they'd like to see their mini-dates again. At night's end, the scores are entered into a computer program that matches up those eager to renew each other's interests. (Three to five matches per person, per party are common, Testani said.)

Strategy, as well as personality, can factor significantly into a person's match rate. Testani and Deckinger recall daters who have handed out resumes, leaned across to kiss their dates, even danced throughout each of their mini-dates.

While noting that some participants go too far, Deckinger said that "differentiation is key in HurryDate. As long as you can stick out from the crowd, you're golden."

Whether any HurryDaters found true love remains to be seen. But for starters, Testani and Deckinger said their main goal is giving participants opportunity to meet people and, if nothing else, enjoy themselves.

"We want it to be fun and hip and attract great people—and be something that we would want to do too," Testani said.

---

first thoughts

like:

dislike:

agree:

disagree:

don't get it:

---

think

- What is your response to HurryDate? Would you be willing to sign up for the program? Why or why not?
- What appeals to you about this sort of dating program? What do you dislike about it? Have you or someone you know tried any dating services, online or otherwise? What have the results been?
- Why do you think it can be so hard to meet someone? What factors in society have led people to use these kinds of dating services?
- Why do you think so many people are in a hurry to get married? When are you the most tempted to put pressure on yourself to get married soon?

pray

read As for the Future

James 4:13-15

And now I have a word for you who brashly announce, "Today—at the latest, tomorrow—we're off to such and such a city for the year. We're going to start a business and make a lot of money." You don't know the first thing about tomorrow. You're nothing but a wisp of fog, catching a brief bit of sun before disappearing. Instead, make it a habit to say, "If the Master wills it and we're still alive, we'll do this or that."

first thoughts

like:

dislike:

agree:

disagree:

don't get it:

think

- Why is it so easy to get caught up in a relationship? In what ways does being a Christian present unique challenges in dating, courting, or considering a future with someone?
- Why is it easy to begin dreaming of a wedding when a relationship is still young?
- How can you maintain a healthy outlook on a possible future with someone when you're just getting to know each other?
- At what point in a relationship should a couple have a "DTR (Define the Relationship)" talk?
- What steps can you take to keep God at the center of your relationship with someone?

pray

read Hooking Up

From "The Cheap Trade" by Stephen W. Simpson[3]

A recent article in a popular Christian magazine took colleges to task for failing to separate the sexes. The author, a Christian professor, railed against his university for allowing co-eds to share the same dormitory and stay in each other's rooms all night. He said that the university was failing to act in *loco parentis* with such permissiveness. He also claimed that boys and girls running amok in one another's dorms resulted in a phenomenon called "hooking up."

"Hooking up" is the twentysomething version of the one-night stand. It occurs when a man and a woman who aren't dating make out or have sex. They are usually friends, though sometimes they just met. Often, copious amounts of alcohol have been consumed. Such encounters seldom signal the beginning of a committed relationship. At best, the couple goes back to being "just friends" the next morning. At worst, they're embarrassed, chagrined or wondering through a hangover why there's a stranger in their bed.

I first heard about hooking up when I was a college freshman in the late '80s. The upperclassmen at my school swooped in, swiped every interesting girl in my class and took them back to their rooms for hook-up sessions. Not only did it ruin any shot I had at a love life, it taught me that most people didn't date in college. They hooked up with strangers in their dorm rooms and then acted as if nothing happened. This was the kind of crap that passed for romance.

When I arrived at college, there was one "experimental" co-ed dorm. During the week, men were banished from the women's dorms at 10 p.m., midnight on the weekends. By the time I graduated, there was only one single sex dorm (a women's dorm), and men and women were allowed in each other's rooms 24 hours a day. As a result of these changes, guess what happened to the frequency of hooking up?

Nothing.

People were hooking up just as much when men and women had their own curfew-protected dwellings. It was a little harder, but not much. All you needed was a "cool" RA or a lover who was willing to hide in the closet when the "not cool" RA came to check the room. Rush the visitor out the back door before dawn, and hooking up was no problem. In fact, it was more appealing. Getting away with hooking up made a guy feel like Neo hacking into the Matrix. When people could come and go as they pleased, I got the sense they didn't enjoy it as much.

Not that I disagree with the professor who thinks college administrators have lost their minds. I hated having women in my dorm. I didn't want to worry about the girls when I was trying to relax or study. And, given my roommate's penchant for locking me out of the room when I went to take a shower, I would have preferred that the ladies had their own crib. Separate dorms also send a message that the university respects privacy and at least pays lip service to sexual morality. However, people don't hook up because of easy access; they do it because they don't have the patience, courage and self-respect to pursue genuine intimacy.

When I became a therapist in a university counseling center and found that hooking up was still alive and well, I resolved to find out why people preferred it to dating. The first thing I realized was that the sexual revolution and changing gender roles made the rites of courtship antiquated. The man used to be the pursuer and the woman the pursued. He was expected to prepare for a career in college, and she was expected to find a husband. Not anymore. The upside of the sexual revolution is that women now get the respect they deserve (most of the time) as scholars and achievers. However, the dating model hasn't adapted. Rather than modifying dating to accommodate modern gender roles, college students often chuck the whole process and cut to the sex.

Though it's becoming harder to delay gratification, it's becoming easier to delay commitment. College students, male and female, often begin a career before they get serious about relationships. The demands are also higher. A bachelor's degree carries the same weight that a high school diploma did 50 years ago. College students need advanced degrees or extra work experience in order to stand out. This leaves less time and energy for dating. However, the needs for intimacy (not to mention blood-boiling hormones) still cry out for attention. Hooking up provides temporary relief of these needs. Just like drugs and alcohol, it meets a short-term need while diminishing the capacity for genuine fulfillment and damaging the person. In this sense, hooking up is the crack cocaine of intimacy.

But the most insidious thing that keeps hooking up alive and well is a poor foundation for closeness and self-esteem. As rates of abuse and divorce continue to increase, fewer adolescents entering college experience stable, loving families as children. This results in young adults with low self-esteem who believe that relationships are volatile and fleeting. Making matters worse, feelings about identity and intimacy solidify during late adolescence and early adulthood. People are figuring out who they are, what makes them loveable and what fulfills them in relationships. If you doubt your value or the security of relationships, hooking up becomes very alluring.

Physical intimacy provides a tangible, immediate sensation of being important to someone else. When you're making out, it *feels* like you're loveable. It doesn't matter if you just met the person or if it's someone who annoys you when the sun is up. Sexual closeness tells your brain that genuine intimacy is occurring, whether it's true or not. Hooking up provides temporary relief from loneliness and anxiety. It's so powerful that you could lock college students in single-sex dungeons and they'd still find a way to get their hook-up fix.

Yes, Christians do this, too. They might be less prone to brag about it, but they hook up all the time. So what are Christian singles to do? The answer sounds simple, but it's not: date.

Somehow, dating has gone awry in the Church. We don't know how to approach it anymore. Old courtship rituals are too formal, and *Sex and the City*–style carelessness violates God's plan. Josh Harris' *I Kissed Dating Goodbye* and Elisabeth Elliot's *Passion and Purity* inspired a fluttering resurgence of courtship among evangelicals, but the restrictions were too many for some. At the other extreme, Christians fall into the world's pattern of kissing their way through opposite-sex friends until they find one they might want to date. Whatever happened to dinner and a movie? What about asking someone out and the slow build-up of romance? Maybe Christians have grown impatient like the rest of the world. Maybe their sexuality scares them into having "friends" instead of boyfriends and girlfriends. But if singles are going to meet their needs for intimacy and avoid the quick and dirty hook-up, they need to date.

The technique is easy. Ask someone out. Respect yourself enough not to kiss someone unless they've earned it by spending time with you and expressing serious interest. Be intentional about making plans with someone you like. That's the easy part; the hard part is having patience and courage. You need patience to find someone special enough to kiss. It takes patience to delay physical intimacy instead of making a "booty call." You need courage to tolerate the uncertainty that dating involves. It takes courage to talk about feelings instead of playing tonsil-hockey.

But Christians are lucky in this regard. If you're looking for a source of patience and courage, He lives inside your heart. God will not only sustain you, He can love you like no one else can. "For as high as the heavens are above the earth, so great is His love for those who fear Him" (Psalm 103:11). If you trust Christ, He'll remind you of your importance and value. The Guy became a human being, lived in poverty, died a grisly death and fought His way back from the dead because He's nuts about you. That's the kind of love you deserve, love that "always protects, always trusts, always hopes, always perseveres" (1 Corinthians 13:6). Give God a chance to remind you of that. It will reveal hooking up for what it is: a cheap trade for unconditional love. It's settling for less. Once you see yourself as God does, you'll settle for nothing but the best.

---

first thoughts

like:

dislike:

agree:

disagree:

don't get it:

---

think

- Why do you think hooking up is so common among young adults? Why is there such a temptation to hook up with someone? What are the advantages and disadvantages to this kind of relationship?

- What do you think about "kissing friends," friends who kiss without commitment? Have you ever been involved in this kind of relationship? How did it make you feel about yourself and the other person? How did things turn out? How do you view that relationship now?

- Why do you think Christians sometimes have a difficult time with the dating issue? What does the Bible say about dating and courtship? Do you think the practices of the ancient days still apply today?

pray

read Is That a Technical Foul?

1 Corinthians 6:12-20

Just because something is technically legal doesn't mean that it's spiritually appropriate. If I went around doing whatever I thought I could get by with, I'd be a slave to my whims.

You know the old saying, "First you eat to live, and then you live to eat"? Well, it may be true that the body is only a temporary thing, but that's no excuse for stuffing your body with food, or indulging it with sex. Since the Master honors you with a body, honor him with your body!

God honored the Master's body by raising it from the grave. He'll treat yours with the same resurrection power. Until that time, remember that your bodies are created with the same dignity as the Master's body. You wouldn't take the Master's body off to a whorehouse, would you? I should hope not.

There's more to sex than mere skin on skin. Sex is as much spiritual mystery as physical fact. As written in Scripture, "The two become one." Since we want to become spiritually one with the Master, we must not pursue the kind of sex that avoids commitment and intimacy, leaving us more lonely than ever—the kind of sex that can never "become one." There is a sense in which sexual sins are different from all others. In sexual sin we violate the sacredness of our own bodies, these bodies that were made for God-given and God-modeled love, for "becoming one" with another. Or didn't you realize that your body is a sacred

first thoughts
like:
dislike:
agree:
disagree:
don't get it:

place, the place of the Holy Spirit? Don't you see that you can't live however you please, squandering what God paid such a high price for? The physical part of you is not some piece of property belonging to the spiritual part of you. God owns the whole works. So let people see God in and through your body.

think

- Does the man or the woman in a relationship have the greater responsibility to preserve his or her body as a "sacred place" in a relationship, or do both parties share the responsibility equally? Why?

- How do you know where to draw the line in a physical relationship? How do you know when you've gone too far? What have you done in those situations to make things right?

- Reflect on this statement: "Just because something is technically legal doesn't mean that it's spiritually appropriate." How does that principle apply to both physical and emotional boundaries in a dating relationship?

- Do you think more damage is done by going too far physically or emotionally in a dating relationship? Why? Which do you think wounds more deeply?

pray

live   The Redefining

Take a few moments to skim through the notes you've made in these read-ings. What do they reveal about the way you handle romantic relationships? Based on what you've read and discussed, is there anything you want to change?

What, if anything, is stopping you from making this change?

Do you have any baggage or unhealthy behavior patterns that tend to follow you from relationship to relationship? Make a list. Share at least one with the members of your group.

How much pressure do you put on yourself to find "the one"? What is the result of this excess pressure or lack of pressure? What can you do to develop and maintain healthy expectations regarding a romantic relationship?

Talk with a close friend about all of the above. Brainstorm together about what it might take to move toward God in this area of your life. Determine what this looks like in a practical sense and then list any measurable goals you want to shoot for here. Review these goals each week to see how you're doing.

marriage material

Love never gives up.
Love cares more for others than for self.
Love doesn't want what it doesn't have.
Love doesn't strut,
Doesn't have a swelled head,
Doesn't force itself on others,
Isn't always "me first,"
Doesn't fly off the handle,
Doesn't keep score of the sins of others,
Doesn't revel when others grovel,
Takes pleasure in the flowering of truth,
Puts up with anything,
Trusts God always,
Always looks for the best,
Never looks back,
But keeps going to the end.

1 Corinthians 13:4-7

a reminder

Before you dive into this study, spend a little time reviewing what you wrote in the previous lessons' Live sections. How are you doing? Check with your small-group members and review your progress toward the specified goals. If necessary, adjust your goals and plans and then recommit to them.

the defining line

This popular passage from 1 Corinthians doesn't just remind us of what true love looks like; it also reminds us of how we are supposed to act in a loving relationship. At a certain point in a romantic relationship, the question of marriage is going to be raised. Before you get to that point, it's wise to ask yourself, *Am I really ready for marriage? Am I ready for a lifelong commitment through thick and thin?* Explain your answer to these questions in the space that follows.

Do you think anyone is ever really ready for marriage? Why or why not?

Do you consider yourself "marriage material"? Why or why not? In what areas do you need to mature before you'll be ready for marriage?

Consider sharing your responses with your group when you meet.

read The Changing Rules of Marriage

From "The M Word: What's the Rush?" by Justin Ellis[1]

Graduation gown to wedding gown. That's how it went, simple as that.

Marriage used to be the next step after school, whether it was high school or college. Like breakfast, lunch and dinner, marriage happened. Tradition dictated it.

But not anymore. The rules are changing. We talk about it among friends. Now the numbers reflect: Young people are delaying marriage much more than generations before them.

Census figures for 2003 show a dramatic difference in the number of couples in their 20s getting married today than 30 years ago. The numbers show what we all know is true. But the reasons are still a little hard to follow.

Talking with young people in the Portland area, one thing is clear: Marriage is not an immediate priority. Now's the time to figure out careers, where you want to live, who you want to know, and who you want to be. That whole "life" thing.

Marriage can wait.

"Getting married isn't so much repulsive as it is impractical," said Joanna Hibbard, a 24-year-old who works in banking. "I don't think it's an awful thing, but it doesn't make sense."

Hibbard has other plans for herself right now, such as travel. She's not waiting to find a life partner to pursue her interests. "I don't think I know someone who could bop around continents with me and could succeed financially," she said.

Hibbard, a Portland native, has a degree in arts administration and French, she's already worked overseas, and sees big things for the "right now." Marriage is not one of them. It's further off, in the future, she admits. There are just a few things she wants to get done first.

"It's about freedom and choice," she said. "I think you have a lot more to offer if you spend more time as an individual with your dreams and goals."

According to the census, 36 percent of women and 55 percent of men age 20 to 24 in 1970 had never been married. In 2003 that figure was up to 75 percent for women and 86 percent for men.

Already there are labels popping up for the generation that seems slow to commit, such as "twixters" or "thresholders."

But Heidi Hart, 27, says her sights are on navigating jobs and career, paying bills, making friends and, most importantly, taking care of herself.

"People don't get out of high school and get jobs that support a family anymore," she said.

Hart said young people watched and learned from their parents, who endured high divorce rates over the past two decades.

The National Center for Health Statistics said the U.S. divorce rate reached a high of 5.3 per 1,000 Americans in 1981, then declined to 4 per 1,000 in 2001.

Hart is a first-year law student at the University of Maine School of Law. She has ambitions of helping people in areas like civil rights and women's rights. She said young people, and women in particular, feel a need to be independent and take care of themselves.

Hart has a special perspective; she became a mother at the age of 16. It changed her way of seeing the "romantic idea" of marriage. She did not marry her daughter's father.

She says her experience made her realize that if she is going to get married, there are certain goals—such as her career and a nice home—that she'd like to reach first.

Look around. You're more likely to see groups of single friends hanging out than married types at this age.

"The single lifestyle is a little more respected than it was before," she said. "It doesn't necessarily mean something's wrong with you."

first thoughts

like:

dislike:

agree:

disagree:

don't get it:

think

- Why do you think so many people are waiting until later in life to get married?
- Do you think older generations have a hard time understanding the delay in marriage? Why or why not?
- For those of you who are single, what are some of the best things about the single lifestyle? How do your married friends view it? What do they miss about it?

pray

read Married a Little Later

From "Ethan's Top Five Things to Tell Your Parents When You Are Still Single at Age 30 (or 35, or 40)" by Ethan Watters[2]

1. "Mom/Dad, among people my age, my life is not abnormal. (At least, not for that reason.) My generation has delayed marriage longer than any generation in American history. The cities are filled with people my age who are still single. The vast majority of us will marry; we'll just do it later."

2. "Not being married does not mean that I'm a 'slacker.' A slacker is usually defined as 'someone who shirks work or responsibility.' Remember how hard I work at my job/school/local SPCA office? My life is full of activity and meaning. There is no reason for pity or scorn."

3. "Despite your stunningly deep bench of candidates, I honestly don't need your help. I'm sure the son/daughter of Aunt Molly's dentist is polite and well-groomed with a high-paying job, but leave the matchmaking to me. Believe me when I say that I have plenty of people giving me advice about my love life."

4. "My marriage delay doesn't mean you won't ever be grandparents. While much has been made of the drop in fertility rates among women over 30, the numbers aren't all that bad. Two out of three women ages 35 to 40 can get pregnant within a year. Those who try for two years raise their odds to 91 percent."

5. "Don't take this the wrong way, Mom and Dad, but what about all the divorces in your generation? People my age are not indifferent to marriage—and we're certainly not indifferent about love—but we have learned

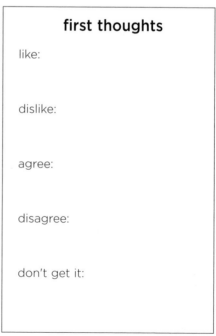

first thoughts

like:

dislike:

agree:

disagree:

don't get it:

to be deeply cautious, in part because of divorce in our own families or those that happened next door. Statistics have shown that marriages started after age 25 work out better in the long run. In fact, because of our marriage delay, the divorce rate is now going down."

think

- What kind of pressure do you feel to get married? Where does the pressure come from? How do you react?
- How do you respond to someone who continually asks you about your romantic relationships?
- Have you ever felt defensive regarding your singleness? If so, describe the situation.
- What are the advantages of getting married later in life? What are the disadvantages?
- Why do you think older generations struggle with twentysome-things marrying later?

pray

read Wives and Husbands

Ephesians 5:21-33

Out of respect for Christ, be courteously reverent to one another.

Wives, understand and support your husbands in ways that show your support for Christ. The husband provides leadership to his wife the way Christ does to his church, not by domineering but by cherishing. So just as the church submits to Christ as he exercises such leadership, wives should likewise submit to their husbands.

Husbands, go all out in your love for your wives, exactly as Christ did for the church—a love marked by giving, not getting. Christ's love makes the church whole. His words evoke her beauty. Everything he does and says is designed to bring the best out of her, dressing her in dazzling white silk, radiant with holiness. And that is how husbands ought to love their wives. They're really doing themselves a favor—since they're already "one" in marriage.

No one abuses his own body, does he? No, he feeds and pampers it. That's how Christ treats us, the church, since we are part of his body. And this is why a man leaves father and mother and cherishes his wife. No longer two, they become "one flesh." This is a huge mystery, and I don't pretend to understand it all. What is clearest to me is the way Christ treats the church. And this provides a good picture of how each husband is to treat his wife, loving himself in loving her, and how each wife is to honor her husband.

---

first thoughts

like:

dislike:

agree:

disagree:

don't get it:

---

think

- Why is marriage so important? What does marriage do for people?
- According to this passage, what are the qualities in a husband that a woman should be looking for? What are the qualities in a wife that a man should be looking for?
- What does a marriage between two people who love Jesus look like? How should wives and husbands treat each other?
- What is the mystery described in the last paragraph of this passage? In what ways should marriage be a reflection of God's laws and love?

pray

read Should You Marry Your Best Friend?

From "The Science of a Good Marriage" by Camille Chatterjee[3]

If anyone understands the chemistry of a good marriage, it's John Gottman, Ph.D. For over three decades, Gottman has interviewed almost 700 couples, recording their interactions and monitoring their heart rate and stress levels in his "Love Lab"—an apartment outfitted with video cameras and sensors. The co-director of the Seattle Marital and Family Institute (with wife and fellow psychologist Julie, also a Ph.D.), Gottman has compiled his well-studied strategies for beating breakups in a new book, *The Seven Principles for Making Marriage Work* (Crown, 1999).

"At the heart of my program," writes Gottman, a University of Washington psychology professor, "is the simple truth that happy marriages are based on deep friendship. By this I mean a mutual respect for each other's company," plus an intimate knowledge of each other's quirks, likes and dislikes. This explains his surprising finding that frequent fighting is not a sign of a bad marriage (unless, of course, it becomes physical abuse). Because while all couples argue, it is the spouses who are friends first who have the advantage.

Amicable partners are less combative during shouting matches than spouses who don't understand each other. And couples who don't respect or have little connection with one another engage in "negative sentiment override"—they interpret statements more pessimistically and take comments more personally than other pairs, leading to dissatisfaction.

Spouses who are friends also make more "repair attempts" dur-

---

first thoughts

like:

dislike:

agree:

disagree:

don't get it:

ing a spat; they say or do things—like make a silly face or bring up a private joke—that keeps anger from escalating out of control. The key point, Gottman reports, is that partners who know each other better know best what will relieve tension in sticky situations—so the fighting stops and the marriage goes on (perhaps) happily ever after.

think

- What would you say great marriages are based on? In what ways does Gottman's study surprise you? How does it compare to other things you've heard or read about marriage?
- Do you think the findings of this article should affect the way people approach relationships? If so, how?
- Why do you think "deep friendship" is so important to a healthy marriage?
- Can you think of any couples this article describes? If so, list them below.

pray

read To Be Married

Genesis 24:32-51

So the man went into the house. The camels were unloaded and given straw and feed. Water was brought to bathe the feet of the man and the men with him. Then Laban brought out food. But the man said, "I won't eat until I tell my story."

Laban said, "Go ahead; tell us."

The servant said, "I'm the servant of Abraham. GOD has blessed my master—he's a great man; GOD has given him sheep and cattle, silver and gold, servants and maidservants, camels and donkeys. And then to top it off, Sarah, my master's wife, gave him a son in her old age and he has passed everything on to his son. My master made me promise, 'Don't get a wife for my son from the daughters of the Canaanites in whose land I live. No, go to my father's home, back to my family, and get a wife for my son there.' I said to my master, 'But what if the woman won't come with me?' He said, 'GOD before whom I've walked faithfully will send his angel with you and he'll make things work out so that you'll bring back a wife for my son from my family, from the house of my father. Then you'll be free from the oath. If you go to my family and they won't give her to you, you will also be free from the oath.'

"Well, when I came this very day to the spring, I prayed, 'GOD, God of my master Abraham, make things turn out well in this task I've been given. I'm standing at this well. When a young woman comes here to draw water and I say to her, Please, give me a sip of water from your jug, and she says, Not only will I give you a drink, I'll also water your camels—let that woman be the wife GOD has picked out for my master's son.'

"I had barely finished offering this prayer, when Rebekah arrived, her jug on her shoulder. She went to the spring and drew water and I said, 'Please, can I have a drink?' She didn't hesitate. She held out her jug and said, 'Drink; and when you're finished I'll also water your camels.' I drank, and she watered the camels. I asked her, 'Whose daughter are you?' She said, 'The daughter of Bethuel whose parents were Nahor and Milcah.' I gave her a ring for her nose, bracelets for her arms, and bowed in worship to GOD. I praised GOD, the God of my master Abraham who had led me straight to the door of my master's family to get a wife for his son.

"Now, tell me what you are going to do. If you plan to respond with a generous *yes*, tell me. But if not, tell me plainly so I can figure out what to do next."

Laban and Bethuel answered, "This is totally from GOD. We have no say in the matter, either yes or no. Rebekah is yours: Take her and go; let her be the wife of your master's son, as GOD has made plain."

---

first thoughts

like:

dislike:

agree:

disagree:

don't get it:

---

think

- Why do you think God made it so clear that these two were to be married? Do you think He always makes it clear when two people are supposed to marry? Can you think of other biblical instances when it wasn't as clear?

- Do you think God has only one person out there for everyone? Why or why not?

- What guidelines does the Bible place on whom you should marry? Why does it place these guidelines? Do you think any of them are outdated?

pray

live   The Redefining

Take a few moments to skim through the notes you've made in these readings. What do they tell you about your readiness for marriage? Based on what you've read and discussed, are there any areas in which you want to change or grow?

What, if anything, is stopping you from making these changes?

Is there anything in your life—unforgiveness, sin, jealousy, anger—that is preventing you from going deeper in your relationships with others? If so, spend some time talking to God about this.

What are you doing to build authentic community, including healthy friendships, in your life? How could you be more intentional about your relationships?

Talk with a close friend about all of the above. Brainstorm together about what it might take to move toward God in this area of your life. Determine what this looks like in a practical sense and then list any measurable goals you want to shoot for here.

Even though you've reached the end of this discussion guide, your progress toward building healthy relationships in all areas of your life should continue. Commit to discussing your goals and discoveries with small-group members or friends as you attempt to live a God-infused life every day.

discussion group
study tips

After going through the study on your own, it's time to sit down with others and go deeper. A group of eight to ten is optimal, but smaller groups will allow members to participate more.

Here are a few thoughts on how to make the most of your group discussion time.

Set ground rules. You don't need many. Here are two:

First, you'll want group members to make a commitment to the entire eight-week study. A binding legal document with notarized signatures and commitments written in blood probably isn't necessary—but *you* know your friends best. Just remember this: Significant personal growth happens when group members spend enough time together to really get to know each other. Hit-and-miss attendance rarely allows this to occur.

Second, agree together that everyone's story is important. Time is a valuable commodity, so if you have only an hour to spend together, do your best to give each person ample time to express concerns, pass along insights, and generally feel like a participating member of the group. Small-group discussions are not monologues.

Meet regularly. Choose a time and place and stick to it. No one likes showing up to a restaurant at noon, only to discover that the meeting was moved to seven in the evening at so-and-so's house. Consistency removes stress that could otherwise frustrate discussion and subsequent personal growth. It's only eight weeks. You can do this.

Think ahead. Whoever is leading or organizing the study needs to keep an eye on the calendar. No matter what day or time you pick, you're probably going to run into a date that just doesn't work for people. Maybe it's a holiday. Maybe there's a huge concert or conference in town. Maybe there's a random week when everyone is going to be out of town. Keep in communication with each other about the meetings and be flexible if you do have to reschedule a meeting or skip a week.

Talk openly. If you enter this study with shields up, you're probably not alone. And you're not a "bad person" for your hesitation to unpack your life in front of friends or strangers. Maybe you're skeptical about the value of revealing the deepest parts of who you are to others. Maybe you're simply too afraid of what might fall out of the suitcase. You don't have to go to a place where you're uncomfortable. If you want to sit and listen, offer a few thoughts, or even express a surface level of your own pain, go ahead. But don't neglect what brings you to this place—that desperation. You can't ignore it away. Dip your feet in the water of brutally honest discussion and you may choose to dive in. There is healing here.

Stay on task. Be wary of sharing material that falls into the Too Much Information (TMI) category. Don't spill unnecessary stuff. This is about discovering how *you* can be a better person.

Hold each other accountable. The Live section is an important gear in the "redefinition" machine. If you're really ready for positive change—for spiritual growth—you'll want to take this section seriously. Get personal when you summarize your discoveries. Be practical as you compose your goals. And make sure you're realistic as you determine a plan for accountability. Be extraordinarily loving but brutally honest as you examine each other's Live sections. The stuff on this page must be doable. Don't hold back—this is where the rubber meets the road.

frequently asked questions

I'm stuck. I've read the words on the page, but they just don't connect. Am I missing something?

Be patient. There's no need for speed-reading. Reread the words. Pray about them. Reflect on the questions at the bottom of the page. Consider rewriting the reading in a way that makes sense to you. Meditate on one idea at a time. Read Scripture passages in different Bible translations. Ask a friend for help. Skip the section and come back to it later. And don't beat yourself up if you still don't connect. Turn the page and keep seeking.

This study includes a wide variety of readings. Some are intended to provoke. Others are intended to subdue. Some are meant to apply to a thinker, others to a feeler, and still others to an experiential learner. If your groove is pop culture, science, relationships, art, or something completely different, there's something in here that you're naturally going to click with, but that doesn't mean that you should just brush off the rest of the readings. It means that in those no-instant-click moments, you're going to have to broaden your perspective and think outside your own box. You may be surprised by what you discover.

One or two people in our small group tend to dominate the discussion. Is there any polite way of handling this?

Did you set up ground rules with your group? If not, review the suggestions in the previous section and incorporate them. Then do this: Before each discussion, remind participants that each person's thoughts, insights, concerns, and opinions are important. Note the time you have for your meeting and then dive in.

If this still doesn't help, you may need to speak to the person who has arm-wrestled control. Do so in a loving manner, expressing your sincere concern for what the person is talking about and inviting others to weigh in as well. Please note: A one-person-dominated discussion isn't *always* a bad thing. Your role in a small group is not only to explore and expand your own understanding; it's also to support one another. If someone truly needs more of the floor, give it to him. There will be times when the needs of the one outweigh the needs of the many. Use good judgment and allow extra space when needed. Your time might be next week.

One or two people in our small group rarely say anything. How should we handle this?

Recognize that not everyone will be comfortable sharing. Depending on her background, personality, and comfort level, an individual may rarely say anything at all. There are two things to remember. First, love a person right where she is. This may be one of her first experiences as part of a Bible discussion group. She may be feeling insecure because she doesn't know the Bible as well as other members of the group. She may just be shy or introverted. She may still be sorting out what she believes. Whatever the case, make her feel welcome and loved. Thank her for coming, and if she misses a meeting, call to check up on her. After one of the studies, you may want to ask her what she thought about the discussion. And after a few meetings, you can try to involve her in the discussion by asking everyone in the group to respond to a certain question. Just make sure the question you ask doesn't put anyone on the spot.

During our meeting time, we find ourselves spending so much time catching up with each other — what happened over the previous week — that we don't have enough time for the actual study.

If the friendships within your group grow tight, you may need to establish some time just to hang out and catch up with one another. This is a healthy part of a successful discussion group. You can do this before or after the actual study group time. Some groups prefer to share a meal together before the study, and other groups prefer to stay afterward and munch on snacks. Whatever your group chooses, it's important to have established start and finish times for your group members. That way, the people who are on a tight schedule can know when to show up to catch the main part of the meeting.

At our meetings, there are times when one or two people will become really vulnerable about something they're struggling with or facing. It's an awkward thing for our group to try to handle. What should we do?

This study is designed to encourage group members to get real and be vulnerable. But how your group deals with those vulnerabilities will determine how much deeper your group can go. If a person is sharing something that makes him particularly vulnerable, avoid offering a quick, fix-it answer. Even if you know how to heal deep hurts, cure eating disorders, or overcome depression in one quick answer, hold your tongue. Most people who make themselves vulnerable aren't looking for a quick fix. They want two things: to know they aren't alone and to be supported. If you can identify with their hurt, say so, without one-upping their story with your own. Second, let the person know you'll pray for him, and if the moment is right, go ahead and pray for him right then. If the moment isn't right, then you may want to pray for him at the end of the meeting. Walking through these vulnerable times is tricky business, and it's going to take a lot of prayer and listening to God's leading to get you through.

Some group members don't prepare before our meetings. How can we encourage them to read ahead of time?

It can be frustrating, particularly as a leader, when group members don't read the material; but don't let this discourage you. You can begin each lesson by reading the section together as a group so that everyone is on the same page. And you can gently encourage group members to read during the week. But ultimately, what really matters is that they show up and are growing spiritually alongside you. The Redefining Life studies aren't about homework; they're about personal spiritual growth, and that takes place in many ways—both inside and outside this book. So if someone's slacking on the outside, it's okay. You have no idea how much she may be growing or being challenged on the inside.

Our group members are having a tough time reaching their goals. What can we do?

First of all, review the goals you've set. Are they realistic? How would you measure a goal of "Don't be frustrated at work"? Rewrite the goals until they're bite-sized and reasonable — and reachable. How about "Take an online personality test" or "Make a list of what's good and what's not-so-good about my career choices so I can talk about it with discussion group members" or "Start keeping a prayer journal." Get practical. Get real. And don't forget to marinate everything in lots of prayer.

notes

Lesson 1

1. A. W. Tozer, *The Pursuit of God* (Camp Hill, Pa.: Christian Publications, 1993), pp. 47-48.
2. Kate Zorichak, "Tips on Surviving Complacency University," *Relevant*, n.d., http://www.relevantmagazine.com/article.php?sid=4757.
3. Mike Yaconelli, "The Glory of Being Stuck," *YouthWorker Journal*, http://www.youthspecialties.com/articles/Yaconelli/stuck.php.

Lesson 2

1. Caroline Hsu, "Tribal Culture: Single But Not Alone, These Urbanites Are Redefining the 'Adultescent' Years" *USNews.com*, October 13, 2003, http://www.usnews.com/usnews/culture/articles/031013/13tribes.htm.
2. Hara Estroff Marano, "The Dangers of Loneliness," *Psychology Today*, August 21, 2003, http://cms.psychologytoday.com/articles/pto-20030821-000001.html.
3. Ellen J. Langer, "I'll Be There," *Psychology Today*, August 2, 2002, http://cms.psychologytoday.com/articles/pto-20020802-000024.html.

Lesson 3

1. "Parents Struggle with Letting Go of College Kids: As Teens Leave Home, Baby Boomer Parents Can't Seem to Say Goodbye," *ABC News*, November 30, 2004, http://abcnews.go.com/GMA/AmericanFamily/story?id=291480&page=1.
2. Linda Greider, "Hard Times Drive Adult Kids 'Home': Parents Grapple with Rules for 'Boomerangers'," *AARP Bulletin*, December 2001, http://www.aarp.org/bulletin/yourlife/Articles/a2003-06-26-hardtimes.html.
3. Linda Perlman Gordon and Susan Morris Shaffer, *Mom, Can I Move Back in with You? A Survival Guide for Parents of Twenty-Somethings* (New York: Tarcher/Penguin, 2004), p. 171.

Lesson 4

1. "Learning to Live with Your Roommate(s): Connections: These Are the People in Your Neighbourhood," *McMaster University*, http://housing .mcmaster.ca/Roommates.htm.
2. LaTonya Taylor, "A Bruised Heart and a Beaten Couch," *ChristianityToday. com*, April 7, 2005, http://www.christianitytoday.com/teens/ newsletter/2005/bym50407.html.

Lesson 5

1. Angela Pirisi, "The Downside of Diversity," *Psychology Today*, November/ December 1999, http://cms.psychologytoday.com/articles/pto -19991101-000013.html.
2. Margaret Feinberg, "Okay, What *About* Bob?" *InterVarsity Student Leadership*, http://www.intervarsity.org/slj/fa98/fa98_cs_bob.html.
3. Andy Crouch, "Extended Family Values: Why Married and Single Families Need Each Other," *The Ooze*, September 5, 2002, http://www.theooze .com/articles/article.cfm?id=100&page=1.
4. J. R. Rushik, "I Hate Stupid People," *Relevant*, n.d., http://www .relevantmagazine.com/article.php?sid=254.

Lesson 6

1. Camille Chatterjee, "Can Men and Women Be Friends?" *Psychology Today*, September/October 2001, http://cms.psychologytoday.com/articles/ pto-20010901-000031.html.
2. Erica Williams, "Can Platonic Relationships Really Exist?" *The Hilltop*, October 24, 2003, http://www.thehilltoponline.com/media/paper590/ news/2003/10/24/NationWorld/Can-Platonic.Relationships.Really .Exist-538029.shtml.
3. Chatterjee.
4. Margaret Feinberg and Leif Oines, *How to Be a Grown-Up: 247 Lab-Tested Strategies for Conquering the World* (Nashville: W Publishing, 2005), pp. 22- 23.

Lesson 7

1. Carla Jean Whitley, "The Six-Month Dating Experiment: Part Two: Addressing My Neuroses," *Relevant*, n.d., http://www.relevantmagazine .com/article.php?sid=6090.
2. "Ready, Set, Date! HurryDate Offers Prospect of Romance in Four Minutes Flat," *CNN.com*, March 2, 2005, http://www.cnn.com/2005/ US/02/14/hurrydate.otr/index.html.
3. Stephen W. Simpson, "The Cheap Trade," *Relevant*, n.d., http://www .relevantmagazine.com/article.php?sid=5844.

Lesson 8

1. Justin Ellis, "The M Word: What's the Rush?" *Portland Press Herald* (Portland, Maine), January 31, 2005.

2. Ethan Watters, "Ethan's Top Five Things to Tell Your Parents When You Are Still Single at Age 30 (or 35, or 40)," *Urban Tribes*, http://www.urbantribes.net/ethans_top_five/index.html.

3. Camille Chatterjee, "The Science of a Good Marriage," *Psychology Today*, September/October 1999, http://cms.psychologytoday.com/articles/pto-19990901-000006.html.

OWN YOUR FAITH.

Redefining Life: My Purpose

Do you know people who truly believe their life matters? If so, you probably notice that this belief affects everything they do. This raises a deep question for the rest of us: What makes the difference between merely being alive and realy living? In this discussion guide, you will be challenged to ask yourself some tough questions about your significance—and where you find it.

TH1NK   1-57683-827-7

Redefining Life: My Identity

So who are you? Only you can know. And part of the journey of self-discovery is God-discovery because He's the One who fashioned you. There is freedom in knowing who you are, and this discussion guide will help you with the process. You'll not only discover what you were created for but also learn about the One who created you.

TH1NK   1-57683-828-5

Redefining Life: My Career

Written for twentysomethings entering the workplace, this study helps you navigate tough job interviews, survive office politics, understand cubicle etiquette, and learn how to represent Christ in your new environment.

TH1NK   1-57683-887-0

NAVPRESS®
BRINGING TRUTH TO LIFE
www.navpress.com

THiNK®

Visit your local Christian bookstore, call NavPress at 1-800-366-7788,
or log on to www.navpress.com to purchase.

To locate a Christian bookstore near you,
call 1-800-991-7747.